PROBLEM SOLVERS

15
INNOVATIVE
WOMEN ENGINEERS
AND CODERS

P.J. HOOVER

CHICAGO
REVIEW
PRESS

Published by Chicago Review Press Incorporated
814 North Franklin Street
Chicago, Illinois 60610
ISBN 978-1-64160-638-7

Library of Congress Control Number: 2022938847

Cover design and illustrations: Sadie Teper
Interior design: Nord Compo

Printed in the United States of America
5 4 3 2 1

For my parents,
the best role models anyone could ever ask for

Contents

Introduction

Hey there, and thank you for reading *Problem Solvers: 15 Innovative Engineers and Coders*! I've had a ton of fun writing this book, and I'm super excited to share it with you. But who am I and why am I qualified to write this book? Well, I'm a writer. And an engineer. Turns out you can be both, though I never realized this when I was younger.

Growing up, the first thing I wanted to be was a Jedi. After all, who wouldn't want to be able to travel in space, use telekinesis, and do cool mind tricks? But seeing as how that wasn't going to happen (I tried—trust me), I spent my summers reading science fiction and fantasy books and teaching myself to program in BASIC on my Commodore 64. For those who don't know, that's a really old home computer— one of the first and, in my opinion, definitely the most awesome. I always wanted the Atari system, but my dad didn't want me playing video games all day, even way back then. But don't worry, I still managed to play plenty of video games on the Commodore 64. *Q*Bert, Jumpman,* and *Castle Wolfen-stein* were some of my favorites. I still manage to play quite a few video games these days, and *Q*Bert* remains one of my favorites.

As for my family, my dad was a pilot and an aeronautical engineer, and my mom was a secretary turned supermom who used power tools and built shelves and never let anything stand in the way of what she wanted to accomplish. In short, I had two pretty great role models, and I grew up loving math and science and building and creating.

What I didn't do when I was younger? Write books. I learned early on that books were things other people wrote, so I contented myself reading about worlds created by J. R. R. Tolkien, Roger Zelazny, David Eddings, and Isaac Asimov, to name a handful.

In school, I straddled the line of nerdiness and the "popular crowd" by spending my days as captain of the varsity cheerleading squad and my nights watching reruns of *Star Trek* and *The Twilight Zone.* I took computer science and astronomy in high school and snuck off to the Smithsonian National Air and Space Museum to watch IMAX movies every chance I got. I took profile tests to see what my perfect career path would be, and given my love of fixing things and my skills at math and programming, engineering seemed a great choice.

When it came to what kind of engineer I wanted to be, it was always an aerospace engineer. My dad was an aeronautical engineer, and I was fascinated by outer space and the idea of exploring strange new worlds (I blame it on *Star Trek*). But then, during my junior year in high school, the space shuttle *Challenger* blew up, killing all seven people on board. I remember watching the explosion while on a ski trip in Vermont. It was so cold that day that everyone was hanging out inside the lodge, and the news kept showing it happen, over and over again. It was horrific, and the tragedy had a pretty detrimental effect on the current aerospace market. I decided that possibly aerospace wasn't the best choice at that time. Instead, I headed off to a college called Virginia Tech where I enrolled in computer engineering.

Computer engineering as a degree was pretty new back then. Of engineering fields, it was the one least represented by females. I was one of four women in the entire class (which was only about forty kids). I took a combination of engineering and computer science courses. I wrote lines and lines of computer code. I wrote video games for my class projects (look for me on Scratch, at https://scratch.mit.edu/users/triciajh/. You can find my games there). And I loved every minute of it. Coding was like problem solving to the extreme. I loved trying new ideas, testing them, and then refining my programs to get them to work. And at the end of four years, I earned my bachelor's degree in computer engineering.

Then, in a strange turn of events, I decided at the end of four years that I wanted to be an archaeologist (just like Lara

Croft and Indiana Jones). I wanted to discover things like King Tut's tomb and hidden cities under the Roman Forum. I'd seen the King Tut treasures the first time they came through America back in 1977, and I'd loved ancient history ever since. So I stuck around Virginia Tech for an extra year and earned a bachelor of arts degree in history. Ancient history, specifically. I loved trying to unlock those mysteries of the past.

But then, once again, things changed, because I figured out engineering might provide better as a career path for the future. I applied to graduate school and continued on at Virginia Tech to get my master's degree in electrical engineering, specializing in digital design.

I graduated, moved from Virginia to Austin, Texas, and got a great job at Motorola designing computer chips. I worked on designs for video communications systems and memory controllers. I was able to live temporarily in Chicago for a year, working at Motorola headquarters. Then, after seven years at Motorola, I switched to Intel, where I continued designing computer chips. The chips I worked on when I was at Intel went into the earliest smartphones and e-book readers like the Kindle. It was exciting cutting-edge technology, and I was thrilled to be a part of it.

Engineering was great. I had friends at work. I enjoyed my job. It paid well. But after fifteen years as an electrical engineer designing computer chips I went through another turning point. I'd just given birth to my second kid, and I wanted to try something different than engineering, but I wasn't sure what.

First, I learned to solve the Rubik's Cube (you should learn to do the same—people will think you're super smart; there's a video of me doing this on YouTube). Then I memorized a really long poem called "Kubla Khan" by Samuel Coleridge (impressive at parties; there's also a video of me doing this on YouTube). And then I got a crazy idea. I decided to write a book. (There is no video of me doing this on YouTube.)

But here's the thing: I was working full-time engineering, and I had two young kids at home (a newborn and a three-year-old). Where would I find the time to write a book? I was washing bottles and changing diapers, all while trying to get a promotion at work. Does it sound impossible? Does it sound like I'd have no spare time whatsoever? That wasn't the case at all. I just had to reassess my life to find the time I needed.

I gave up television. All of a sudden, in the evenings after the kids' bedtimes, I had a good two hours on my hands, and I used it faithfully each night to write my first story. Four pages at a time, and after three months, I had a completed first draft. It's amazing what you can accomplish if you chip away at it a little bit at a time. In case you are interested, my first book is called *The Emerald Tablet*, and it's about kids with telepathic and telekinetic powers—the exact powers I wanted when I was younger! It's the first book of a trilogy about kids from continents hidden under the ocean called The Forgotten Worlds.

People tend to think of engineering and writing as totally different fields, but they have a lot in common. Getting through engineering school requires discipline and organization. Writing a book requires discipline and organization. Designing computer chips takes quite a bit of creativity. And yes, we all know writing a book takes creativity. Computer code is a lot like a book. You write. You test. You revise. You test some more, and you keep on revising until you get it right. Sure, you might find bugs, but no computer chip is perfect. Neither is any book.

So that gets us to here, with me writing this book featuring fifteen amazing female engineers and coders. This book was like a dream come true for me, like a melding of my two worlds. For each and every woman featured in this book, I was able to interview them on a one-on-one basis. I connected with them on so many levels. Being a working mom juggling all life's day-to-day activities while trying to stay in shape, managing a house, and still getting my job responsibilities done. Learning how to say no and to delegate and to lead teams. It was like I'd found my people once again. It was truly an honor to interview these women, and I'm thrilled to have the privilege of sharing their stories with you.

This book features the stories of fifteen women who have defied the odds, who have found a way to attend college even when there was no money, who have broken out of abusive relationships, who have spoken up for themselves even when no one would listen. These women are on the cutting edge of technology. From renewable energy to cancer research, these women are changing the world. They're making it a better place for all of us. And they are paving the path for more female engineers and coders by being amazing role models and mentors. I hope you find as much inspiration in their stories as I have.

Part I
Against the Odds

Gabriela A. González: Find a Way

Have you ever been told you can't do something? How many times does it take to be told you can't before you start to believe it? And why do these voices sometimes come from the most trusted sources, our teachers and counselors and parents? For Dr. Gabriela A. González, these voices were an integral part of her life. She was told over and over that she wasn't good enough. That she should give up on her dreams.

What if you didn't have to listen to the voices or believe them? What if you knew there were wonderful options out there for you? What if never considering yourself "good at math and science" didn't hold you back from being an engineer? So often the study of engineering is reserved for the "kids who are good at math and science," but that doesn't have to be the case. Many boys consider STEM fields because it's a known and encouraged option for them. But for the vast majority of girls, it's only the ones who have been told by teachers that they should consider engineering who go on to pursue it. Dr. Gabriela A. González is on a mission to change this.

Gabriela was born in Mexico and lived there until she was 13, but then her mother divorced her dad and moved with her five children to Harlingen, Texas, a town in the Rio Grande Valley near the border. While in Mexico, Gabriela's family was considered middle class. The schools provided a good education, Gabriela worked hard and excelled, and she planned to go to college. This was a true possibility for her.

However, her college dreams were shattered with the move to the United States. Money was scarce. The family was on welfare, lived in public housing, and worked hard to scrape by. And as immigrants from Mexico to southern Texas, Gabriela felt discriminated against, even though she had the same skin color as her peers. There were defined classes in society, and in these classes, Gabriela and her family were at the bottom.

Gabriela's mother sold everything they owned and moved the family to Washington a couple of years later. Here, Gabriela, her mother, and her siblings picked crops in the fields to get by. Gabriela babysat and found a job in a daycare. She continued with school and worked when not studying. The family lived in public housing and lived off welfare and food stamps. College was becoming a distant fantasy in Gabriela's mind. Then, when it seemed things couldn't get any worse, the car crash happened.

While driving, another car sideswiped the family car and sent it tumbling down an embankment. Thankfully, everyone survived, but Gabriela's mother broke her neck. The driver of the other car didn't have insurance, and Gabriela's mother was out of work while she recovered. This was one more crushing blow against Gabriela's dreams for college.

Though Gabriela always wanted to go to college, she never had her mind fixed on engineering specifically. She did well in math and science and enjoyed art and history and many things. She knew a higher education would be valuable in life, and despite so many setbacks, she couldn't give up on the dream.

College Is an Option

College is a great step toward a secure future, but growing up, some may feel like college is an impossibility. It's easy to rule out going to college for any number of reasons. It may be too expensive for some. For others, their grades may not be good enough. It could be too far away from home. Some kids may feel too scared. Too shy. Maybe no one in their family has ever been to college before. Kids may not have the luxury to wait to earn money but feel the need to earn a paycheck now. Or maybe they're sick of school and don't want to study anymore. But for each of these reasons, there are solutions.

Yes, college can be expensive, depending on where you want to go. But programs exist to help. Scholarships and financial aid are available. Work-study programs are common at many schools, offering jobs for those in financial need. Flexible class hours are available, allowing students to work while also taking classes. Will it be easy to work and study at the same time? No. The bad news is that people can't do everything all at once. Time management becomes really important, and concessions are going to have to be made. It might be the case that football games or parties have to be skipped. But the good news? Working while going to college can make college affordable.

What about grades? There are all sorts of colleges in the world. Many colleges mean many options. Applying to a school can't hurt. Good advice may be to apply to other colleges besides your first choice. Even if you don't get into your first-choice college or the degree you want to pursue, you can transfer or change course later if your grades are good enough. Get into college. Work hard on your grades. And then apply for the major you are interested in.

If the thought of moving away from home is too much to handle, consider other options. Take classes at a local college. Many urban areas have community colleges that will help you get credits toward your degree. And if you really want to just earn some money, then start small. Take one class at the community college. Maybe two. This will give you plenty of time to work also, allowing you to get a paycheck while working toward your college degree.

After facing discrimination at the church they were attending, Gabriela's family switched churches, attending services on a nearby Native American reservation where their skin color fit in better. There, Gabriela met a youth counselor who had just graduated from the University of Washington with a chemical engineering degree. At this point, Gabriela had pretty much accepted that she would have to work after graduating high school to save up enough money for college if she ever wanted to go. But the youth counselor brought her to the university and introduced her to people in the engineering department. They offered her a scholarship, and Gabriela's dreams for college became a reality.

What Is a Mentor?

Mentoring is a term lots of people like to throw around, but what is it really and what does it involve? The idea of mentorship has been around for a long time, actually since ancient Greece. In Homer's famous poem The Odyssey Athena assumes the appearance of Odysseus's trusted companion Mentor, whom he had left to look after his son, Telemachus, while he was off at war. The guide's role is to give advice and support to Telemachus. Whether the story is true, the idea of a mentor has stuck around for thousands of years. Athena was the first mentor.

In simple terms, a mentor is somebody who provides advice, guidance, and support. This can be in either a personal or a professional sense. If you've ever considered looking for a mentor for a career field you may want to enter, there are some key things to keep in mind. You may need to approach someone and ask if they'd be willing to mentor you, or you may be approached and asked if you'd like a mentor. Neither is the wrong path but it's important to be as informed as you can be.

In a good mentor-mentee relationship, there are some critical components: First, finding the right mentor is important. If you are looking for a mentor, make sure to do your research when it comes to who you might want to work with. Before you approach the person, know what they do—not just what job they work at but what specifically they *do*. If you're hoping to work with an electrical engineer, keep in mind that is a broad field. What does your mentor do specifically? Do they design computer chips? Run a product line? Program computers? If you can, dig deeper. If they do design computer chips, what types of products are those chips used in? Some information may not be accessible, but it's good to do a thorough search. Has the person been interviewed? Participated in podcasts or panels which may be available to listen to? It's flattering to know that someone has taken the time to get to know about you specifically.

Another important element is to have defined expectations for what the mentoring relationship will involve. Does it require meeting once a week or once a month? Does your mentor assign you tasks or use your meeting times to teach you about the business? A mentor will be more likely to agree if the commitments are known and not too consuming.

What if someone approaches you and asks if you'd like a mentor? So many people want to give back to the community, and mentorship is a great way to do that. Having someone offer to mentor you is a great opportunity, but you want to make sure you are ready for a mentor. Are you willing to meet at the expected times? Do any work your mentor may assign? If not, don't think that means your future is over. It may not be the right time for you, but sometime in the future you may be ready for a mentor.

And on a final note, once you are an adult and in the working world, consider being a mentor yourself. You absolutely have something to offer others, and it truly is a great way to give back to the community.

Her entire life, Gabriela was told by counselors, teachers, other adults, and even her peers that she couldn't do what she wanted to do. She was told she wasn't good enough. That she didn't have the money. That she should get married and have a family instead of pursuing her education. But Gabriela refused to believe these voices. If anything, she wanted to prove them wrong. Even once in engineering, Gabriela was encouraged to study what were considered the "easier" engineering fields. She was told fields like computer and electrical engineering were too hard for girls. This only made Gabriela more motivated to succeed.

According to Gabriela, so many girls are told, "You can't do that because . . ." And after hearing this enough, they begin to believe it. The message gets reinforced as they get older, and when it's time to make a decision about their futures, so many girls never consider higher education. Or if they do plan to go to college, they never consider engineering because "they aren't good at math and science."

According to Gabriela's research, girls *are* being introduced to STEM. However, as she noted, only about 10 percent of girls are being introduced through current programs. These are the girls who are "good" at math or "good" at science— meaning that they get high test scores out of the gate or have received some extra help from parents or tutors. These are the ones who have been tapped on their shoulders by their teachers or counselors. Gabriela wants the other 90 percent of girls to also have that introduction, to know that a future in engineering or computer science is an option. And so many of the girls who are being overlooked are being counseled away from STEM fields. Girls whose families are on welfare, who can't afford tutoring or math camp. Girls who don't have the highest grades in math. Girls who become teen mothers. Girls who have to work while they're in school. Girls who never believed in the possibility of higher education or a field like engineering.

In 2005 Gabriela launched a nonprofit program to reach these girls called Hermanas (Sisters in STEM). It offers a day camp to underrepresented girls to introduce them to STEM with hands-on activities where girls can experience for themselves how fun STEM can be. It has an education fair, which is kind of like a job fair but for after-school activities. And it has town hall meetings where speakers will come in and give the message that girls can be engineers. They can be computer scientists. And Gabriela is particular about which speakers she chooses. Their past experiences—what they'd been through—matter most to her. She's brought in teen mothers who have gone on to get engineering degrees. She's brought in students and professionals who lived on food stamps or worked in the fields picking crops like she did, or those who worked to help support their families or who didn't do well in math in high school. These are the kind of role models needed to reach this other 90 percent of girls.

The main message Gabriela would love to get across? Engineering and computer science are real options. Just because you aren't good at something right now doesn't mean you can't be. So many girls can be engineers. They just need to learn to believe it and see themselves doing it.

Today, Gabriela is a deputy director at Intel and continues to run Hermanas (Sisters in STEM). In addition, she is on the board of the National Girls Collaborative Project and Project Lead the Way. She is also chair of the NSF STEM Education Advisory Panel. She is fascinated by ancient history and loves to travel. When she retires, she would love to continue her work helping change the landscape of girls in STEM. Girls can do anything, and Gabriela is determined to prove it.

Aztec and Mayan Pyramids and Engineering Techniques

One of the reasons Dr. Gabriela A. González loves ancient history is because when she travels to archaeological sites she can imagine what life used to be like. She can think about the engineering techniques that went into building structures that are standing thousands of years later. Some of her favorite sites to visit are the ancient pyramids in Mexico. Both the Aztecs and the Mayans populated Mexico centuries ago, and both left lasting architectural achievements.

Perhaps the most famous of the Mayan pyramids is on the site of Chichén Itzá in Mexico's Yucatán Peninsula, which was built around AD 600. El Castillo, a large step pyramid, dominates the site, standing nearly 100 feet (30 m) tall. Archaeologists believe construction may have taken place over the course of hundreds of years.

Ancient Mayan engineers did not have access to modern tools, but that didn't stop them from figuring out how to build breathtaking structures. They had no metal tools but instead crafted chisels from obsidian and black jadeite, which they used to carve out the stone blocks for their structures. They didn't use a unit of measure but proportioned their buildings according to universal laws of nature like the golden ratio. Instead of a base-10 (decimal) number system like we use, their engineers used a base-20 (vigesimal) system for calculations needed for construction.

The next time you're faced with a project and you encounter a problem, think back to the Mayan engineers and the challenges they faced. If they could figure out how to build entire pyramids without metal tools, then maybe you can solve your problem too.

Sue Black:
Take Control

When Sue Black walked into her first computer science class in her late twenties, sporting red hair and Doc Martens, to say she stood out is an understatement. But then nothing so far had placed Sue on the traditional path to becoming Dr. Sue Black, professor of computer science.

Sue's somewhat average life took a turn for the worse when she was twelve years old and her mom died. Her dad remarried . . . too soon, and not to the right person. Sue's home life quickly became a place of emotional and physical cruelty and severe neglect. There was never enough to eat. Her and her siblings' clothes were never clean, and what clothes they owned had holes in them. Sue reached her limit when she was 16. She confessed to a friend what was going on at home, and her friend suggested Sue move in with them. Sue packed half her belongings and moved out. When she went back home a week later for the rest of her stuff, her dad had already burned whatever was left in a large bonfire out back.

Sue found her new circumstances beyond everything she could have imagined. Living at her friend's house, Sue felt like she was permanently on vacation, because everything was so much better than it had been at home. That said, Sue did have to do her part with chores and had to pay rent. Between attending school, working to make money for rent, and washing up around the house, some nights Sue couldn't start her homework until after midnight. This soon became an unsustainable situation, so she dropped out of school and began working full-time.

But what to do? Both her parents had been nurses, so Sue tried her hand at that. But as an extremely shy person, she found nursing wasn't quite the right fit. Actually, she despised it. She then got a job working in the accounts department for a record company. Aside from cool music, this job involved lots of math, which Sue found she enjoyed quite a bit.

Life changed once again for Sue when she got married at the age of 20. She soon had three kids (one girl and twin boys). But as the marriage progressed, her husband became more and more abusive. Sue felt trapped, and things were only getting worse. When the twins were about one and a half (around the time Sue was 25), her husband came home and, after an extremely harsh argument, he threatened to kill them. He'd been verbally abusive before, but he'd never gone to this extreme. Sue packed all their stuff in one suitcase, put the twins in a double buggy, and with her daughter holding on to the handle of the stroller, she left home, hurrying to a friend's house. But her husband knew where she was. He called on her friend's phone and threatened them once again. Sue, worried for their lives, hurried to another friend's home. Her friend gave her taxi money, and by that evening Sue and her kids were safely in a women's shelter.

Escaping an Abusive Situation

Nobody should have to stay in a dangerous or abusive situation. Sue Black feared for her life and the life of her children. She was able to call a friend to help and make her way to a women's shelter. But what should you do if you or someone you know is trapped in an abusive situation?

If you are in an abusive situation, the most important thing to realize is that you deserve better. You deserve healthy relationships in your life, and you are not trapped. You are not to blame for the situation, and you are not responsible for abusive behavior. Whether you are watching someone you love be abused or whether you are the one suffering, you can do something. Create a plan and act on it.

The first thing to do if you are in an abusive situation is to tell a trusted adult. This could be a school counselor, a teacher, a school nurse, or a friend's parent. Sometimes it's hard to talk about this kind of thing in person. You can write a note or send an email or a letter. Unless you tell someone, things may never change, so even if you are scared, this is an important first step to take. Abusers will not change their behavior, no matter how much you may want them to. Even if they promise to stop, they won't. The statistics are real. You can't change them. You need to change this situation and do what you can to get yourself and your loved ones to safety.

In the event you don't have a trusted adult you feel you can talk to, know that there are resources out there to help you. There are crisis hotlines you can turn to. There are many resources available online where you can call and ask for advice or help. However, oftentimes, abusers will be able to access Internet search records. If you don't feel safe searching this on your home Internet or your phone, ask a friend to search or call for you. Use a computer at the library. Go to a safe location and call using a friend's phone.

If you or someone you love is in danger, called 911 and make sure to give your name and location. Don't hesitate. The abuse needs to end. You deserve a better life.

Once Sue's kids started school, Sue wanted to get a job to support herself, but she soon found out that she didn't have many qualifications. Not sure what else to do, she signed up for a math class at a local college. There was some computer programming Sue didn't fully understand, but she still kind of liked it. So she decided to officially enroll in college for a computer science degree.

Life was challenging. With three young kids, there were many times Sue thought about dropping out. She had to pick up her kids by two o'clock each day. She would miss lectures while taking care of them. Sue frequently went to her personal tutor's office crying and saying she was going to quit, and each time he would encourage her to stay. Despite the odds, she stuck to it and graduated four years later.

During her last year of undergraduate studies her supervisor asked if she'd like to get a PhD. Sue had no idea what a PhD was, but she pretended to know and said, "Oh, I'd love to do a PhD." She applied and was accepted. A normal PhD in computer science takes around three years to complete. Sue took seven years. But at the age of 39 she officially became Dr. Sue Black.

What Is a PhD?

When Sue Black was advised by a mentor to continue on and get her PhD, she eagerly agreed. It sounded like a fantastic opportunity. The problem was that she didn't know what a PhD actually was. She did some research and discovered that, yes, her mentor was correct. Pursuing her PhD would be a wonderful career choice. But what is a PhD exactly, and should you consider getting one?

Generally, when someone goes off to college, it is for a four-year undergraduate degree known as a bachelor's degree. This can be in any of a broad range of subjects. In some fields the next step in education is applying to graduate school and earning a master's degree. This often takes two years and can be a specialization built on whatever degree was earned as an undergraduate. Though this means six years of college has now been completed, for those looking to earn a PhD, there is still more on the road ahead.

A PhD, which stands for "doctor of philosophy," is the highest-level degree that can be awarded. In order to earn this degree, you need to produce advanced work that makes a significant contribution to your field. But why is "philosophy" part of the name? It's not because you're going to be sitting around thinking all the time. *Philosophy* in ancient Greek translates to "loving wisdom." So, if you intend to earn a PhD, it's assumed you love studying the area you are specializing in.

Earning a PhD will take a minimum of three more years. In addition, candidates will need to research and submit a thesis, which is a paper that shows the research you've been doing and presets the conclusions. You'll then need to defend this in what is known as a dissertation. Once you do this and pass, you can officially use the prefix *Dr.* before your name.

Getting entry to a PhD program doesn't grant you immediate acceptance in the world of academics. Sue, who was still very shy, would attend conferences and try to network. She found that these conferences were mainly populated by men, and they weren't necessarily interested in talking with her. She got ignored. She got stared at. It wasn't the welcoming experience she'd been hoping for. Then she went to a Women in Science conference, and her eyes were opened to an entirely different world. Everyone was talking to everyone. It was warm and welcoming, and it changed her life.

Sue realized that when you're with people from similar backgrounds—whether that means gender, skin color, or ethnicity—life is easier. She wanted to do what she could to help other women in the field, so in 1998 she set up the UK's first online network for women in tech. But Sue's passion didn't stop there. In the early 2000s she ran a campaign to save Bletchley Park, the site of the Allied codebreaking in World War II. When Sue visited the site, she learned that over 8,000 women worked at Bletchley Park during the codebreaking efforts, yet there was nothing about these women or their contributions anywhere. She vowed to change this, and in 2015 she published the book *Saving Bletchley Park*, the fastest crowdfunded book yet seen.

Women at Bletchley Park

Sue Black's work to save Bletchley Park was largely inspired when she discovered how many women had worked at the site, unacknowledged and nearly forgotten. Bletchley Park was the central site for cryptanalysts during World War II, known most famously for its success in cracking the Enigma machine code. Without this success, the outcome of the war would be unknown.

If a woman wanted to be employed at Bletchley Park, she couldn't just walk up to the gate and ask to fill out a job application. There was a process. First, family connections mattered. Especially of interest were "debs," who were women of the upper class. They were thought to be trustworthy because of their upbringing. But debs and family connections did not always bring in the top talent, especially for something as complicated as codebreaking. The job roles debs filled were mostly administrative and clerical work. What Bletchley Park needed were women who were linguists, mathematicians, and crossword experts. In 1942 a newspaper known as the *Daily Telegraph* hosted a cryptic crossword competition that had to be solved in 12 minutes or less. In a cryptic crossword, each clue was a word puzzle itself. Women who were able to solve the puzzle in the allotted time were recruited to work at Bletchley Park. They were thought to have the skills needed for codebreaking.

When these women arrived in Bletchley Park, despite their skills or credentials, some men doubted they would be capable of operating the complex machines used for codebreaking. They were assigned to jobs such as index card compilers, administrators, or messengers. But when given the opportunity to prove themselves, the skills of many of these women were soon recognized. Some were even assigned as codebreaking specialists.

There is now a roll of honor at Bletchley Park, commemorating the names of those who worked so diligently to help win the war. As of now, there are around 8,000 women on that list.

Sue realized that kids needed to start learning tech at a younger age, so she started running workshops for seven-year-old kids (the same age as her youngest daughter at the time). She soon concluded that if kids could learn this stuff, anyone could. According to research Sue had done in her continued pursuit of equity in learning, she discovered that the main positive influences on kids doing well in school at age 11 were the mom's education level and the home environment. So, with this in mind, she put together the #techmums program to teach moms about technology. Sue started running the program at a school in a disadvantaged area in East London. The program changed the way mothers saw themselves. It changed their attitude about technology. But the biggest change was in their self-esteem. They saw themselves as being worth something.

Sue realized that there are a load of women with potential out there, and there are a load of technical jobs. But there aren't many pathways to get those women into those jobs. She created a program to take potential women and match them with technical careers. A woman may start off taking Computer Science 101, but through the program, she will take courses and learn new skills suited to a specific job role. The program focuses particularly on women from underserved backgrounds.

According to Sue, there are so many people out there with potential, but it's really all about opportunity. You may have opportunity in front of your face for years and never realize it. Her program is all about making that opportunity be seen.

One thing Sue wants girls and women of all ages to do is to trust their gut instincts. Girls are often brought up to trust other people's opinions more than their own. Sue Black ended up in some bad places where her life went wrong because she didn't really trust her own feelings. If she'd trusted her gut, how different would her life have been?

She believes girls need to get out there and go for it. When things get in your way, get around them or get through them. Life will give you so many challenges. Everyone has challenges. But the people that are the most successful are the ones that just keep going and overcome those challenges. Even if you have to do something 100 times just for it to be successful once, that's what's going to make you successful. It's normal to get knocked back lots of times. But don't let getting knocked back stop you.

As women, we often think if someone says no once, that's it. We can never ask again. But we need to learn that if you want something, you just keep going until you get it, and you don't take no for an answer.

Sue Black is currently a professor of computer science and technology evangelist at Durham University, where she gives all sorts of speeches spreading the message that if she can do it, you can do it too.

Noramay Cadena:
Take a Chance

Does having a baby when you're only 17 ruin your plans for the future? It doesn't have to. Just ask Noramay Cadena, mechanical engineer and now a managing partner at Supply Change Capital, a powerful venture capital company in Los Angeles and Chicago. The secret for Noramay was finding what she was passionate about and pursuing opportunities that came her way, even when they seemed scary.

Noramay was born in Mexico and moved to Los Angeles with her family as a young child. She grew up in the San Fernando Valley in a community where 97 percent of the students were Latinx, and most families were first-generation immigrants. Sure, she was good at math and science, but she didn't have a strong sense of what she wanted to be when she grew up.

Her high school had more than a decade-long track record of top-performing graduates enrolling at MIT and then paying the service forward by continuing to share their story with high school students and encouraging them to follow in their footsteps. When Noramay heard one of these speakers share his own personal journey and his experience as an engineer, that path suddenly resonated with her and became tangible. Noramay applied to MIT and was admitted.

But the prospect of relocating across the country wasn't so easy for a teen mom who had given birth to her daughter two weeks into her senior year in high school. She questioned whether it made sense for her to move to a place where she lacked family support. But MIT invited her to come out and visit anyway. Noramay had never been outside California, other than family trips to Mexico, but her fear of the status quo life she would lead if she didn't do things differently inspired her to get on the plane and go.

MIT demonstrated that accommodations could be made to support her enrollment and her dual life as a student and parent. There were family dorms available where she could live with her daughter. There was childcare available on campus. MIT did not immediately write her off for having unique circumstances and needs as an undergraduate. And at the end of the visit, Noramay began to realize that maybe it was possible after all. But she had to be willing to leave her comfort zone of California, leave her family and support network, and start on a whole new adventure. Noramay accepted their offer, agreeing to start at MIT in the fall after graduation.

In a community where college away from home was not necessarily the norm, Noramay started getting attention from the local news outlets. At first her dad wondered why she had to go all the way to Boston. Was she not good enough to get into the local California State University? But then her parents started to realize that this was a big deal and a big opportunity. And with the hopes and support of her family and her community behind her, Noramay set out with her daughter to attend MIT.

Could fear have held Noramay back? Most definitely! It was scary leaving her family and support network, especially having a young child, but she had grown up living through experiences she did not want repeated. She had a firm vision of what she did *not* want her life to look like. Her fear of the status quo was much bigger than her fear of moving across the country and doing something unknown. What really drove her was that she wanted something different and wanted to provide for her daughter. She wanted to be independent and wanted to support her parents. It was similar to what her parents did when they came to America. They didn't know what they were getting into, but they knew if they stayed in Mexico, the opportunities available for their children would not yield the future they wanted.

Attending College with a Baby

Having a baby at a young age can make it seem like the rest of your life is already planned out, and yes, it does add an extra complication. Statistics have shown that single mothers earn fewer degrees and leave college with more debt than those who are married or who don't have children. But if college is in your dreams and hopes for the future, it is still an option! Many colleges offer support programs, resources, and amenities for those with young children. These include family housing, financial aid, childcare, and other resources to help women with children be successful while earning their college degrees. The help doesn't necessarily stop there. Many colleges offer goal planning, career assistance, and priority placement for internships and work-study opportunities.

If you're considering attending college and have a young child, look specifically for a college with support. Instead of viewing college as an impossibly hard thing to do, it can be viewed as an opportunity. While Mom is attending classes and studying, children attend camps, go on field trips, participate in fun learning programs, and go to lessons of their own.

The support programs and amenities aren't just about making life easier. Think of the amazing role model these young mothers offer to their children by not letting life get in the way of their career dreams. They want more for themselves and for their children, and that role modeling will help pave a successful path for generations to come.

For the next four years, Noramay studied mechanical engineering. While there, she followed in the footsteps of people she admired, whether that was what to study, what clubs to join, or where to work during the summers. She came to realize that even with this amazing education, she was following, not leading. She did not yet recognize her own power or truly step into it. Noramay hadn't established her own goals or aspirations for college or her job after graduation.

As Noramay gained more experience, she also gained more clarity on what she truly wanted in life. In the first six years with her first employer she'd been promoted five times. She was doing great work at Boeing, but she still felt like a follower and wanted to define her own path. However, in order to do what she wanted, she had to know what that was. At that point, Noramay set a goal to be a leader in operations. She made a plan. Her first step toward this goal would be getting a business degree. With this step, she was no longer following. She was in the driver's seat of her career, picking her own journey. She realized that the people who once intimidated her were not necessarily smarter than she was, and she needed to accept that this was an environment she belonged in.

With the help of her employer, Noramay went back to MIT and enrolled in a dual-degree graduate program where she received both a master's degree in engineering systems and an MBA. Upon graduating, Noramay returned to Boeing and focused on leading large teams building complex space hardware. As she progressed in her career, she found an increased desire to innovate faster. She wanted to innovate quickly and to be part of teams bringing products to market in record time. She wanted something more.

What Is an MBA?

MBA stands for "master's in business administration" and is an advanced degree that focuses on running businesses and managing investments. There's quite a bit of coursework that may be covered while earning an MBA. There is focus on all aspects of a business: communication, ethics, law, and strategy. There are also courses in accounting, finance, human resources, statistics, supply-chain management, operations management, economics, and marketing. That sounds like a lot, but don't worry. Just like with undergraduate degrees, those who pursue an MBA will generally specialize in a particular area.

Earning an MBA takes about two years of full-time schooling. There are other popular options for MBA programs, including taking classes in the evenings while working during the day, and an accelerated program where the course load is heavier but allows for graduation within a year.

After attending college for four years to earn an undergraduate degree, the last thing someone may want to do is go to more college, but a graduate degree like an MBA can definitely pay off. Those with MBAs often go on to get much better and higher-paying jobs, such as investment bankers, portfolio managers, financial analysts, or even founders of their own companies.

Recalling her past, Noramay considered herself extremely lucky to be tapped on the shoulder by an MIT student who suggested there was more opportunity for her out in the world. While in college, she met four other young women who shared that opportunity that changed the course of their lives. Wanting to do the same for other young women, they teamed up to launch the Latinas in STEM Foundation. The five of them began working within their respective communities across the country, but there was so much need to share their stories within underrepresented communities, and Noramay and her friends could only do so much while still working their full-time jobs. They started recruiting other women, which helped, but it was still a lot of work. Through Latinas in STEM, they were able to leverage a network of women across the country. Beyond that work, Noramay wanted to find a way for her passion to help others to converge with her day job.

She really cared about the intersection of innovation, impact, and equity, and with this in mind, she discovered the venture capital sector.

Noramay cofounded the venture firm MiLA Capital, which created an ecosystem in Los Angeles for early-stage founders who were building tech you could touch. For five years, she worked hard to build programming and networks for first-time founders of tech companies in the manufacturing, supply-chain, and logistics space. She got a crash course in venture capital, and the company made 22 investments across sectors like mobility, health, food and agriculture, manufacturing 4.0, and climate tech. When that work was exhausted, Noramay thought about where to focus her efforts next. The answer involved combining early-stage investing with community building and investing in women and underrepresented founders. The introspection led her to investing in food and food tech with a cultural lens.

Noramay is now a managing partner at Supply Change Capital, a venture capital company focused on the intersection of food, culture, and technology. The team invests with a focus on what the table of the future will look like in terms of better-for-you, better-for-the-planet, and culturally relevant brands. The demographics of the United States are shifting. Households are more multicultural than ever, and people are embracing food from other cultures. Noramay and her company are working to create the ecosystems and communities around founders of companies that are not only bringing products and services to the market but also bringing organic foods, allergen-free foods, and other sustainably sourced foods to the table. They want to invest in companies that help build traceable supply chains, pay living wages for farmers, and build cultures that attract and retain talent by offering flexible schedules, growth opportunities, family leave, and a great work-life balance.

What Is Venture Capital?

Venture capital is a term you may have heard, but what is it exactly? Venture capital companies, like Supply Change Capital, are private companies that finance other companies they believe in, in exchange for equity in the company. That means if a venture capital company invests in a company that does well, then the venture capital company and its investors will earn a share of the profits. If the company does not do well or fails, the venture capital company will lose their initial investment.

This sounds like a pretty risky business, and it is. Venture capital-backed companies typically have a high rate of failure. But they're also exciting. Venture capital companies are at the leading edge of discovering the next Uber, Chobani, or Airbnb. In the venture capital market, companies like this, which can reach a market valuation of $1 billion dollars or more, are considered "unicorns." It's the type of company every venture capitalist wants to find early.

A venture capital firm doesn't just write a check and sit back to watch and see what happens. It's often the case that the firm truly cares about the company they're investing money in, and not just because they've put money in it. They want these companies to succeed often because it falls in line with their vision of the future. Sometimes venture capital companies will provide strategic advice on the company's business model and marketing.

Noramay says that a lot of her job is fundraising and travel. She needs to raise the money to invest, and then she wants to meet with the founders of the companies looking for backing. When she meets with these companies, she looks for gaps and helps find ways to support them. She also works to bring more investors into our ecosystem by developing relationships with other investors.

With her focus on food and this notion of the New American Table, she looks for products and technologies that stand out. What's going to be the next Chobani yogurt? What will the next hot protein be? Other countries offer new-to-the-US opportunities to uncover sustainable and better-for-you ingredients and flavors. Beyond investment, the team is creating ecosystems and communities around founders to make them successful. Noramay and her company help by providing not only the financing but also the mentorship, the advisory services, the coaching, and whatever else their clients need to continue to grow and scale.

As for the main thing Noramay Cadena would love to pass on to young girls? Looking back at her life, she hadn't been stepping into her own power. She was following, not creating her own path in life. She was being inspired but not necessarily inspiring. But girls should know that if others can inspire them, then they can inspire others. One person may inspire you in the way they treat people. Someone else may inspire you with their drive. Someone else with the work they do. Soak up as much as you can from others, but ultimately pick and choose what feels right for you, what feels like who you are. Take pieces from other places and form them to be the best version of you.

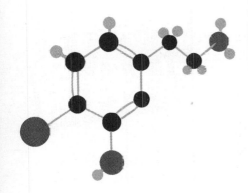

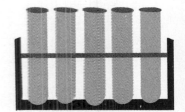

Part II
Cutting-Edge Tech

4

Karmella Haynes:
Change the World

Millions of people are affected by cancer every year. It's a horrible disease with no cure. Cancer cells divide quickly and don't die often enough, making them a deadly enemy. But cancer cells are like any enemy. They have a weakness. What if that weakness could be found and be reprogrammed? What if we could fight cancer cells from the inside out? That is exactly the kind of research genetic engineer Dr. Karmella Haynes is working to make a reality.

Growing up, Karmella describes herself as always being a nerdy kid. She would pluck dandelion petals and wonder how they were connected to each other. She was constantly doing crossword puzzles and solving problems. And she was also very interested in art, so much so that in fourth grade her art teacher suggested that an art tutor might be in order since Karmella always went above and beyond and really tried to push herself. The school simply didn't have the art supplies Karmella needed. So, for four years, Karmella studied art with a tutor, creating her first oil portrait at the age of eleven.

When Karmella was in high school, she saw *Jurassic Park*, and sure, it was entertaining, but Karmella couldn't help but point out all sorts of science gaps in the movie. That was when Karmella decided she wanted to be a genetic engineer. She wanted to go to college and learn as much about genetics as she could.

What's Wrong with *Jurassic Park*?

In June 1993 the movie *Jurassic Park*, based on a book by Michael Crichton, exploded onto the scene and instantly became a blockbuster hit. It made the very cool explanation of science easy for viewers to understand: dinosaurs are cloned by blood found inside mosquitoes trapped inside amber, and an amusement park where guests can see "real dinosaurs" is born. Great idea, exciting premise, but what did *Jurassic Park* get wrong?

Let's start with the time period. Most dinosaurs lived during the Cretaceous period, not the Jurassic. That's not bad science. That's just incorrect marketing, like calling a movie *Gen X* when it's about kids born in the 1990s. But then there is the problem of the DNA. In order to clone an animal, like a velociraptor, you'd need an entire genome.

That would be all the chromosomes that make up the dinosaur. At this point, nobody has found even a little bit of dinosaur DNA, not to mention an entire genome. Will it happen in the future? Maybe. But DNA degrades over time. Dinosaur DNA would need to be 65 million years old . . . and would need to not be degraded at all.

Another issue with the movie is that, at the time of its making, we didn't have the facts on what these creatures really looked like. Some may have been bigger or smaller than portrayed, some more brightly colored, others covered in feathers. Sure, dark-green, scaly dinosaurs look terrifying in the movie, which makes for good cinematography, but it doesn't make for good scientific realism.

Still, as is often the case, entertainment wins out over science, and viewers don't mind. If they did, *Jurassic Park* would not have gone on to become the massively successful franchise that it now is.

But even with Karmella's interest in how things worked on a deep scientific level and her talent in art, college was not a given. Her family was lower-middle class, and neither of her parents went to college. Karmella, who considers herself the family genealogist, recounts how her grandma barely finished grade school, but was determined for her kids to do better. Her mom's family grew up near Duncan, Mississippi, and were tenant farmers. When Karmella's mom was born, there were complications, and the rural colored hospital didn't have the resources to deal with them. Her granddad pleaded with his boss, and with some strings pulled, they were able to go to the White hospital in the main part of town. The baby (Karmella's mom) was delivered safely. But the hospital then charged a large fee, and the boss had no intention of paying it. Instead, he deducted it from the family's small paycheck, making it such that, after all the bills were paid, there was no income left. This wasn't a sustainable situation, and yet they were legally under contract to their tenant farmer boss. So, in the middle of the night, in the 1950s, her mom's family ran away. Although slavery had been abolished over 80 years before then, they literally had to escape in the middle of the night to get out of a tenant farming contract.

As for her dad, he had been hugely interested in STEM. He was in his school's science club, and he dreamed of attending MIT. Even though no one in his family had even gone to college, he went to his guidance counselor and told him about his MIT aspirations. His counselor gave Karmella's dad what she called the "Malcolm X treatment." The counselor told his dad that it was unrealistic. Negroes didn't do that sort of thing, and he needed to be more practical. He did not end up going to MIT.

Still, Karmella's dad was always her STEM hero. When she attended college, studying genetic engineering, she had the opportunity to attend a summer research program at MIT. The first thing she did? Went to the bookstore and bought her dad an MIT T-shirt.

As for art and genetic engineering, can they overlap? Most definitely! In her work, Karmella creates her own graphics, which she admits she spends way too much time doing. But she enjoys it, and she is able to incorporate more diversity into those graphics. Take, for example, one of the key areas Karmella's research focuses on: triple-negative breast cancer. This is the deadliest form of breast cancer and disproportionately affects Black women. When Karmella puts together graphics for presentations and papers, she wants this to be reflected. According to Karmella, it's important to get the right representation in graphics for science and engineering.

What Is Triple-Negative Breast Cancer?

About one in eight women will develop invasive breast cancer in their lifetimes. That's about 13 percent of women. Breast cancer, if caught early, has a huge rate of survival. But there are various types of breast cancers, each with its own survival rates depending on treatment.

A breast cancer cell has receptors on it. These receptors are proteins that are found inside and on the surface of the cell. They receive messages through the bloodstream that tell the cell what to do. There are three main receptors: estrogen, progesterone, and HER2. Estrogen and progesterone are hormones, and about two-thirds of breast cancers test positive for these receptors. About 20 percent of breast cancers test positive for HER2. Therapies that target these hormones or HER2 receptors can be used to slow down or stop the growth of breast cancer cells.

When a breast cancer cell tests negative to all three of these receptors, it is considered triple-negative. This occurs in about 10 to 20 percent of all breast cancers. Triple-negative breast cancer is generally more aggressive and has a lower chance of survival than other types of breast cancers because there are fewer targeted medicines to treat it. Standard hormone therapy or HER2-targeted therapy can't be used since those receptors are not what is instructing the cell on how to grow and divide. Women younger than 50 are more likely to be diagnosed with triple-negative breast cancer, as are Black and Hispanic women.

It's a terrifying thing to find a lump in your breast, but the good news is that there are treatments available and survival rates are good. Today's treatments for breast cancer involve a combination of surgery, chemotherapy, radiation, and targeted drug treatment. The best thing to do is to stay ahead of the problem. Monthly breast self-exams are critical, even from an early age, and as women get older, they should get mammograms to check for any abnormalities. It's better to catch a problem early than to pretend it isn't there.

Karmella's research focuses on how chromatin is used to control cell development in biological tissue. This is a fancy way of saying that she is looking for a way for genes to be turned on and off. For her research with triple-negative breast cancer, the ultimate goal is to get rid of the cancer without needing chemotherapy. Chemotherapy poisons the whole body. It can cause hair to fall out, lead to sickness, and take a heavy toll on a person, not to mention patients often have to sit in a chair with a needle in their arm for hours, which is unpleasant. Currently, this is what the treatment looks like and what gives the best chance of survival. But Karmella believes we can come up with something better.

In her research, she looks at cells. Is there something different about the cancer cells? They are powerful adversaries, but do they have a weak spot? Cancer cells behave differently than normal cells, and Karmella looked for what causes them to behave differently, which goes all the way down to the DNA. If scientists can identity some really specific things inside the cells that make them act differently, and if they can then make a better treatment that only affects that very cancer, then maybe the normal cells will ignore it and not be affected.

All cells—skin, muscle, fat, blood—have different personalities. There is a diversity in cells. Cancer is tissue, but it is bad tissue and doesn't play nice with the rest of the other tissues. So Karmella looks at how the genes are expressed. There are 23,000 genes in the human body, and all of them are expressed differently.

Karmella believes that scientists can change the cells so that their gene expression looks more like normal cells, so they will stop doing things like growing tumors and traveling where they shouldn't in the body. She and her team are trying to reprogram or retrain cancer cells to behave more like normal cells or maybe even die, which is a natural part of cell turnover. Cancer cells divide a lot, but they don't die off enough. So, there is a huge imbalance in how the population is maintained.

Cell Division

Cells are the basic building blocks of life, and your body is filled with nearly 40 trillion of them. They're too small to see with the naked eye but can be seen under a microscope. Every living thing has cells. Some living things are made of a single cell, while others are made of many cells. The cells work together to form your heart, lungs, skin, and every other part of your body. Cell division is what allows a single cell to grow to a multicellular being.

A human being starts with two cells: an egg and a sperm. These are special types of cells used just for sexual reproduction. When the egg and the sperm come together to form a new cell, the cells divide frequently during this embryonic stage. A single cell has a copy of all the genetic material (the chromosomes). When a cell is getting ready to divide, it will duplicate this genetic material and then divide into two cells. Each cell will have a copy of that genetic material, and the two new cells will be identical. This process of cell division is called mitosis.

So, what makes a cell know whether it should be a heart cell, a skin cell, or a cancer cell? Well, think of the chromosomes as a set of instructions on how to build a human. Cells cannot each follow all these instructions. A cell will only "express" or follow certain instructions. One cell will follow the instructions for being a heart cell. Another will follow instructions for being a skin cell. This is called *differentiation*, and it's what allows an embryo to turn into a fully formed human. In the case of Karmella Haynes's research, her team is looking for ways to turn off some of these instructions, thus causing the cells to express themselves differently.

Scientists like Karmella are working with drugs right now to change this gene expression. They are using drugs to go into cancer cells and fight them from the inside. In essence, they are deprogramming the cancerous behavior from the cancer cell.

Karmella Haynes has a message for young girls. When she was younger, she spent way too much time worrying whether she had offended someone. But she's come to learn that, often, if a person responds negatively to something you've done, that is not on you. Don't ever accept the suggestion that someone is trying to convince you that you are doing something wrong. So many people of all ages still have outdated world views, and it's difficult for young girls to navigate society these days. But these outdated views are other people's problems, not yours.

Be the best "you" you can be, and see how you can change the world.

Dr. Karmella Haynes is a biomedical engineer and associate professor at the Wallace H. Coulter Department of Biomedical Engineering at Georgia Institute of Technology and Emory University, where she continues her work on how chromatin can be used to control cell development.

Eva Saravia: Face Life's Challenges

Are all those hours playing video games a total waste of time? Not necessarily! In fact, video games are being used to train soldiers for real-life battle situations. They help them prepare for the unexpected, build their muscle memory, and teach them to work in teams. This is the kind of exciting technology Eva Saravia, senior vice president of global programs at Bohemia Interactive Simulations, has the opportunity to work on each day.

There was never a question whether Eva was going to go to college. Both her parents were first-generation immigrants, from Guatemala in Central America, and from an early age they knew a huge part of living the American dream was hard work and education. Education, especially, they saw as the key factor that set people apart. It had the power to change things for their children and for generations going forward, so they instilled this belief in Eva and her brothers from an early age.

Eva's dad was always fascinated with tech. He would come home from his job as a technician and talk about his work and the people he worked with who were engineers. He wanted this for his daughter. She wanted it for herself. For Eva, it was kind of set that she would be an engineer. The question was what kind of engineer was she going to be.

In middle school Eva was part of a group of kids who took the early bus to the high school to take an advanced math class offered there. The girls in the group all hung out together because their schedules lined up. They became known as the "nerd herd," not in a bad bullying way, but in a fun way, as a compliment. They enjoyed STEM, and they weren't embarrassed about it.

While Eva was in high school, biomedical engineering was the up-and-coming field, and it fascinated Eva. According to her, she worked her butt off because she was determined to go to college back in Boston where she'd lived when she was younger. She applied to Boston University, and because of her hard work, she was not only accepted but also offered a fantastic scholarship package. So long as she kept her grades up, her school would be paid for. But that turned out to be more of a challenge than Eva had expected.

In college, she lost her scholarship. She couldn't keep up her GPA, and now college was no longer paid for. Out-of-state college is expensive, and Eva had to face the hard truth of what losing her scholarship meant. Did this mean that engineering wasn't for her? Should she pack up and go home and figure out something else to do? Or should she find a way to keep going? The answer came down to her goals and her motivation. Eva loved engineering. She wanted to stick with it. And so, Eva worked two jobs, and her parents cosigned loans with her. She kept going, and she never regretted it.

Keeping Your College Scholarship

Colleges offer scholarships for a variety of reasons. Some may be based on the grades or standardized testing scores you received in high school. Some may be based on athletics. Others can be based on the level of your family income. For example, if your household income is below a certain point, there are many colleges out there that will cover most of your college expenses. One thing that is true about all scholarships is that you have to work hard to keep them. There are many reasons why you might lose a scholarship if you receive one, and if a scholarship is lost, it will definitely add a complication to finishing your degree.

Although the reasons for losing a scholarship might vary from place to place, here are some of the possible reasons your amazing scholarship could be taken away.

Keeping your grades up is important! For many scholar-ships, if your GPA (grade point average) falls below a certain point, you risk losing the money. Many scholarships also require students to be enrolled in a certain number of credit hours per semester (12 is pretty common). Using scholarship money for something besides what it is intended for can also get your scholarship revoked. If you receive a scholarship, make sure to read the rules about what you can and can't use the money for.

Colleges also want students to follow rules, and breaking these rules could get your scholarship taken away. Getting caught cheating, drinking underage, or using illegal substances could mean the end of your college dreams. If you receive an activity-based scholarship (like a soccer scholarship) but break your leg and are unable to play, you could be at risk of losing your scholarship. It's also really important to send updates if required. No one wants to bother filling out forms, but if your scholarship requires regular updates on how you are doing, then it is your responsibility to make sure these are done (on time and in a professional manner).

But even after graduating with her bachelor's degree, the path ahead was not easy. In her mid-20s, Eva found herself divorced with two young kids. As a single mom, the easy option would be to play it safe. To not take any challenges. But instead, Eva thought about her future and what her goals were. She decided to go to graduate school in Florida, where she received her master's degree in industrial engineering and engineering management.

In her professional career, Eva has taken opportunities that have helped pave the way to where she is now as a senior vice president at Bohemia Interactive Simulations. She's had some great role models in her life that recognized her potential. They gave her options and advice. Looking back, Eva realizes how important these role models were, and it reflects on how she interacts with her team. She knows that as you advance, you have to give back. Life is not a one-way street.

As a leader who is also a woman of color, Eva realizes how important it is to make sure her voice is heard. Too often, it's easier for women to take a step back and listen instead of being the driving force of a discussion. Women often begin second-guessing themselves before speaking up because speaking up can put them out of their comfort zone. This is an important challenge for women to overcome, especially if they want to be leaders. It's not easy, but women must make themselves be heard. However, a key part of this is that in order to do it well, you must be prepared. You need to know your stuff and not be afraid to bring it up.

Bohemia Interactive Simulations is a military defense company that provides modeling and simulation solutions for military training. They started as a part of a gaming company that used game technology for training, and they have grown and evolved to now serve over 60 countries worldwide to assist with military training.

Benefits of Video Games

Many parents hear about video games and immediately think there is no good that can come from a kid playing them. But there are, in fact, many benefits to playing video games. And there are all sorts of different video games to play. If you happen to be in the category of trying to get more video game playing time, maybe it's worth coming up with a list of the pros in order to sway your parents. Who knows? If your list is good enough, you may even be able to convince your parents to play.

Video games can make you more coordinated. There is a lot of eye-hand coordination needed, and video games improve your manual dexterity. They can also boost your brain connectivity, helping with things like memory, muscle control, and perception. It may seem counterintuitive, but video games can actually improve your social life. Having something like video games in common gives kids something to connect about, and many video games offer collaborative modes where kids can work and play together.

New types of gaming, like virtual reality and augmented reality, can actually make you more active. It's hard to sit on a couch and swing your arms around to fight while evading assassins. They can also help improve problem-solving skills. Some games are all about thinking outside the box in order to advance to the next level. And this problem solving can teach persistence. Gamers may try over and over to solve a problem, which if you think about it, is a very handy life skill. And even from a super early age, video games are a great way to sneak learning into having fun. Whatever it is you want to learn about, a video game takes feeding your brain to a whole new level!

So why video games? Turns out there are some very good reasons Bohemia Interactive Simulations uses game technology. There are also challenges in making gaming technology realistic enough for training.

The great thing about video game technology is that, because of its consumer popularity, the technology development is already being funded in the commercial market. Bohemia Interactive Simulations leverages this tech for their military solutions. In addition, many soldiers have grown up playing video games. They are already used to them, which helps them train as quickly as possible.

But there are some key differences. Bohemia Interactive Simulations simulates military situations like those soldiers may really encounter. They need to make sure to stay focused on realism, and they need to avoid negative training (learning the wrong skills or behaviors). Take a first-person shooter game like *Call of Duty* as an example. In *Call of Duty*, your avatar may never experience fatigue. Though the weather may change in the game, from rain to snow to desert heat, these environmental changes are not taken into account in how they affect the player. What does rain mean in terms of vehicle traction and mobility? What if there is a crowd nearby? What if a field is filled with goats and fencing? The simulations Bohemia Interactive Simulations creates must be highly realistic and precise.

Simulations can use not just virtual reality but also augmented reality. The cockpit of an airplane or the controls of a Humvee can be used, helping troops develop better muscle memory. In simulations, troops can work as teams. They hear each other's voices. They understand radio calls. And everything is recorded, making it easy for teams to review and analyze performance.

What Is Augmented Reality?

Virtual reality is a term many people are familiar with because it's been depicted in so many books and movies, including Ready Player One, Jumanji, The Matrix, and Total Recall. The player puts on a headset, and they are immersed in another world entirely. This science fiction isn't just fiction anymore. All it takes is putting on an Oculus Quest headset, and a family room can be replaced by a fancy 3D lounge with an apps menu that allows users to select games and experiences. (Beat Saber is great and definitely worth trying.) No longer is the real world around them visible. The technology is so good that it's pretty easy to forget what's actually going on around you.

But what about augmented reality? People may have heard the term but not been quite sure what it was. In augmented reality gaming (ARG), a computer-generated image is superimposed over the real world. Think *Pokémon Go*. After downloading the app and giving it permission to use the camera, suddenly the city streets and buildings are full of monsters that need to be captured. Pikachu might be found at the Roman Colosseum. Magikarp could be captured at a coffee shop by the lake. Is *Pokémon Go* not your thing? Don't worry! You can still try augmented reality gaming. Nintendo hasn't been the only one to jump on the augmented reality craze. *The Walking Dead, Minecraft, Jurassic World*, Star Wars, and Harry Potter all have their own entertaining apps you can try out to give the real world around you an entirely new look.

Eva's job is not just video games (though the company employs many types of people, including game testers who get to play the games for a job). She often has meetings all day long. But she keeps as a priority her home life, balancing meal prep, homework, and lunch with her girlfriends.

A key concept that has helped Eva advance to where she is today is to not be afraid to try new things, even when the prospect seems terrifying. She's found new things she's tried have worked out well—for example, scuba diving, an activity her entire family now enjoys, which is a huge accomplishment seeing as how Eva was scared of the ocean for much of her life—and others have not worked out nearly as well—like riding a motorcycle, which Eva quickly determined was not for her.

Eva's main message boils down to perseverance. Life is not easy. It's not supposed to be easy. It is supposed to be challenging. You can look at a challenge as an opportunity for growth and learning and then tackle it. Or you can run the other way. When you're faced with hard choices and decisions, are you going to stick with your plan? If you want to succeed, you have to. And something that can help keep you on track is knowing what your motivation is. Know what your goals are. Know what is the thing that will make you stick to those goals. And when things get hard, when you fall back, take a moment to catch your breath and then keep going.

Lola Eniola-Adefeso:
Set Your Own Path

Chemotherapy is a treatment that uses powerful drugs to kill fast-growing cells in the human body, and it's often used to treat cancer. The problem is that in addition to killing the cancer cells, it often kills others healthy cells also. Hair loss is perhaps the most familiar visible side effect of this. But what if instead of the drugs attacking all the fast-growing cells, they could be targeted such that they only kill the cancer cells? Imagine the reduction in side effects and how much better patients would feel. Sounds too good to be true, but this targeted drug delivery is exactly what chemical engineer Dr. Lola Eniola-Adefeso is working to make possible.

Nobel Prize in Chemistry

Can being a chemical engineer make you famous? Can you win awards? If you are Frances Arnold, American chemical engineer and Nobel laureate, then the answer is yes. Since earning a PhD in chemical engineering, Frances Arnold has racked up quite a list of awards. The most impressive? In 2018 she won the Nobel Prize in Chemistry for her work in directed evolution, giving her the distinguished title of Nobel laureate. Since its beginning in 1901, only seven women have won the Nobel Prize in Chemistry, including Marie Curie, who discovered the elements radium and polonium. In 2020 Emmanuelle Charpentier and Jennifer Doudna were both awarded the prize for their work in the discovery of gene technology's CRISPR/Cas9 genetic scissors, which allow any DNA molecule to be cut at a predetermined location. The winner of the Nobel Prize in Chemistry receives a gold medal, a diploma, and a nice sum of money.

So, what kind of research does it take to win such a prestigious prize? Frances Arnold's work centered on directed evolution. This field of study is when organisms are created with desired traits through a series of iterative rounds of protein modification. It can be performed in living organisms or in cells and is often used to create enzymes that can be used in industrial applications that make the industry more efficient. In short, it speeds up the process of natural selection.

creating organisms with modified traits. Enzymes are used in many reactions because they are natural catalysts, which are substances that increase the rate of a chemical reaction without going through any chemical changes themselves.

Even though the Nobel Prize in Chemistry is pretty impressive (and can make you well-known enough to have a cameo appearance on an episode of *The Big Bang Theory*), it's far from Frances Arnold's only award. In 2011 she received the National Medal of Technology and Innovation, an honor granted by the president of the United States, and in the same year she was the first woman to receive the National Academy of Engineering Draper Prize. In 2016 she won the Millennium Technology Prize, one of the largest technology prizes in the world, also for her work in directed evolution. Truly, the list could go on and on.

Lola grew up in Nigeria in a highly educated family where college was always in the plans. However, with strong gender divides in society, engineering was not an option for Lola. Women were not engineers. They could be medical doctors. They could go into business or art. But they just weren't visualized as engineers. In high school in Nigeria math grades determined the classes students were partitioned into at the time. Lola, being very good at math, was placed in science, which meant her future most likely lay as a medical doctor or as a nurse. But Lola wasn't sure she wanted to be a nurse. She was good at biology, but she didn't find it all that intellectually stimulating. She wanted more. And after she moved to the United States, her options opened up. She took one of those tests on a computer that determines good career choices depending on your strengths. Lola was great at math and chemistry, and the computer suggested that chemical engineering might be a good future. Lola agreed, and it was the best thing that ever happened to her.

When people think of chemical engineering, they often think of the oil and gas industry. Oil and gas may not sound all that attractive, and they certainly seem pretty different from the idea of targeting drugs to help treat diseases like cancer and heart disease, but according to Lola, they aren't all that different at all. Blood is a viscous fluid traveling through pipes just like oil and gas. And it is in that fluid that Lola's research takes place.

What Does a Chemical Engineer Do?

It's true that the first thing most people think of when it comes to chemical engineering is the oil and gas industry, but chemical engineering is so much more!

The technical definition of chemical engineering is that it is a field of engineering that focuses on the production and manufacturing of products through a chemical process. So chemical engineers will come up with and

design new processes involved in chemical manufacturing. But where does this work actually take place?

Chemical engineering touches everything. The computer
chips in our phones and computers have the signature
of chemical engineering inside them. Chemical engineers work in pharmaceuticals and healthcare, helping
refine drugs to make them affordable and available. They
improve the quality and quantity of our food, helping with
food-processing techniques and fertilizer production.
They develop advanced materials and polymers, creating
synthetic fibers for fabric to make it waterproof, fire-
resistant, and comfortable. They work to make energy
and chemicals cost-effective and productive. They also
work on environmental problems, including recycling,
pollution, water treatment, and disease control.

If you take a look around, everything is made up of chemicals. You, the house you live in, the gas in your car, the
clothes you wear, the food you eat. All these chemicals
have been refined to make them as efficient as possible,
and this work will continue in the future. Where do you
think chemical engineering will take us in the future?

Drug delivery is taking a drug into your body. When you
take a pill, you are delivering a drug through your mouth.
If you have a headache, you may take aspirin. If you have
diarrhea, you may take Pepto-Bismol. It goes in your mouth

and into your stomach. The stomach is designed to break things down into their smallest components, and much of the drug gets lost this way. Then, after being broken down, the drug is absorbed into the bloodstream through the stomach wall and intestinal wall. But once it's in your blood, its journey is not over. In your blood, the drug travels through your body. A good chunk of it gets lost in the liver, so you have to take higher doses of the drug because, on this long path the drug needs to take, a lot of it is not getting where it needs to be. The conclusion: drug delivery through the mouth and into the stomach, while convenient, is not the best route. In addition, if someone tried to take poisonous drugs, like chemotherapy drugs used for cancer, orally, it would kill everything in the body. So, what is a better option? Drugs can be inhaled, which gets them into the bloodstream more quickly, but you can only get so much to go deep down into the lungs. Drugs can also be injected directly into the bloodstream, but once again, so much of the drug gets lost in the liver.

This is where the idea of "targeted" drug delivery comes in. In targeted drug delivery, drugs are packaged into tiny little carriers that are too small to see without a microscope. These carriers protect the drug from the elements of the body, making sure they don't get broken down by enzymes that are in the blood or liver. But how do the drugs know where they need to go? How do they know their "target"? It turns out your body is a lot like a nation at war. When a nation is attacked, by an injury or a disease, warning signals are sent out. These signals tell when your liver is not working properly or when a tumor has developed and takes the form of proteins on the surface of a cell. Certain proteins are associated with cancer, others with heart disease. A normal, healthy cell would not have these proteins, but the injured or diseased cell does. What Dr. Lola Eniola-Adefeso's team does is package the drugs to fight the injury or disease into a carrier and then "decorate" the surface of that carrier with proteins or antibodies that will "stick" to the warning signal proteins. These carriers are then injected into the bloodstream and will travel around until they find the right cells to stick to.

That sounds pretty intricate and complicated, but the pros of targeted drug delivery are many. This highly targeted approach gets the drug only to the diseased area, sparing the rest of the body from the effects of it. So, for example, chemotherapy drugs, which currently attack all fast-growing and dividing cells, would attack only cancer cells, sparing hair cells and other healthy cells. This reduces the amount of drug needed, meaning less of the drug gets wasted, which also lowers the overall cost of the drug.

In addition, the carriers can also be engineered to determine how quickly or slowly they break down and release the drug. This could be over the course of weeks or months, meaning the patient wouldn't have to pop a pill three times a day. This improves patient compliance.

Patient Compliance with Medication

Doctors prescribe medications to patients every single day. When you get a prescription, you generally talk to the pharmacist so you know how you are supposed to take the medication. But, despite this, about 50 percent of patients don't take their medications as prescribed. This can put patients' health at risk.

There can be a variety of reasons why a patient does not take medication as prescribed, and healthcare workers employ various strategies to help deal with this issue. Some patients may have dementia, making them simply forget to take the medication. Other patients might be symptom-free, making them believe the medication is no longer necessary. Others still may not be able to afford their medication.

To help with medication compliance, it's important to create a blame-free environment. It is best to get the truth of what the patient is doing when it comes to medication without making them feel guilty for missed doses. Talking about possible side effects ahead of time can help patients continue taking medications even when side effects appear. Medication calendars, schedules, and charts can help keep patients on track. Helping patients understand what is happening with their health is also critical. The more they understand the problem, the more likely they will be to take the medication to help with it. Keeping medication as simple as possible is also important. A once-a-day pill is much easier to remember than something that must be taken three times a day with food. Following up with patients through text and email reminders can help, as can patients having a phone number they can call any time of day or night with questions. In addition, pillboxes help patients stay organized with medication. Some even operate automatically, dispensing pills only when needed. These may even be able to be monitored by healthcare providers through Bluetooth connections.

This sounds amazing, doesn't it? But it's not without challenges. For example, some of the information on the "warning signal" proteins isn't available until after a person has lost their life. You can't remove a diseased blood vessel while someone is still alive, and current imaging techniques are not sensitive enough to zoom in on blood vessels. A tumor can be studied once it's been removed, or a bad artery can be examined after being cut out during a bypass, but this is all after the fact. However, biomarkers, which are indicators of a disease, are shed by the body and can be found in blood, urine, stool, tissue, and other body fluids. When these biomarkers are found, they can be studied and used to advance the research.

The future of medical technology is rapidly expanding, and we are only just beginning to understand how all the technology we have at our fingertips can be used to remove barriers and advance our knowledge. As we get more precise and specialized, with robotics and electrical fields, a world of possibilities begins to open up for researchers like Lola.

But research wasn't always what Lola had planned to do. It wasn't until she was in graduate school that her future changed. While at a conference, a research adviser asked Lola to have breakfast, during which she asked Lola if she had ever considered being a professor. The research adviser thought Lola would be great at it and remarked that they could use more people who were smart and motivated like Lola in academia. At this point, Lola hadn't even really considered what she wanted to do. She was in graduate school because she wasn't ready to get a job and be an adult yet. But Lola loved the intellectual stimulation and creative freedom that graduate school gave her. So she decided to take the research adviser's advice and applied for a faculty position. Once she did this, she never looked back.

Lola wants every girl to recognize herself as an individual and not to let anybody else set their path. Every girl has self-worth, and the path girls take should be driven by them, not by external forces or societal norms. She encourages girls to embrace who they are, celebrate their gender, and recognize that there are strengths that they bring to the table by being a woman. Lola loves being a woman. She never hides the fact. And she finds that with that attitude of embracing who she is, there is a lot she can do.

Dr. Lola Eniola-Adefeso is the university diversity and social transformation professor of chemical engineering, biomedical engineering, and macromolecular science and engineering at the University of Michigan, where she enjoys starting each day with a long jog and a hot cup of coffee.

Part III
Leading the World

Danielle Merfeld:
Just Ask

Can taking one small action change the entire path of your future? Will you even recognize it when it happens? When Danielle Merfeld walked into the engineering department at the University of Notre Dame and asked for a job her freshman year of college, she didn't know it would change her life. She just wanted to be able to satisfy her work-study commitment to help pay for college, and in order to do this, Danielle needed a job. Colleges have all sorts of job opportunities. Danielle thought that working in a laser lab sounded pretty cool, so she took a chance.

There were a few very interesting things about this incident. First, taking such a forward action was out of character for Danielle, who considered herself somewhat of a quiet and shy teenager. Second, Danielle didn't think the engineering dean would say yes when she asked. He did. And third, Danielle found herself working alongside students who were pursuing their PhDs. At first this was intimidating. But soon she realized that these other students, though working toward advanced degrees, were no different than she was. And if they could get a PhD, what was to say that she couldn't also?

This small inspired action changed the course of Danielle's life. After earning her undergraduate degree in electrical engineering from the University of Notre Dame, she went on to earn her PhD in the same field from Northwestern University.

Upon graduating, Danielle went to work for General Electric, having no idea that she would be there for the next twenty years. At GE an opportunity quickly came her way to move into a leadership position. Danielle could have said no. She could have come up with excuses for why she wasn't qualified. But instead, she took the opportunity, and her success grew from there.

Using her success for good, aside from the immense technical responsibilities Danielle has in her job at GE Renewable Energy, she is also a huge advocate of drawing more women to technical fields and to leadership roles. She fosters leaders, both female and male, both by taking actions and by providing them with a strong role model.

Leadership opportunities bring up a whole issue with society and the drive for perfection that many women struggle with. Studies by Catalyst, a global nonprofit company that works to be inclusive and to help advance women in the workplace, have shown that women demand much more out of themselves than men before even applying for a job. For example, if a job posting lists ten required skills, men will, on average, apply for the job if they only have two or three of those skills. Women on the other hand will hold off on applying for the job unless they meet nine or all ten of the listed requirements. As a result, far fewer women apply for the jobs, and thus far fewer women are hired for these positions.

But women aren't the only ones holding themselves back. Danielle also notes another problem with job postings themselves. The very wording of a job posting could be off-putting to women, often using sports terms or more aggressive language that may appeal more to men. At GE she identified the problem and worked to get it changed. She notes that there are issues at every level with drawing women into technical careers and leadership, and she is on a mission to change these.

Danielle Merfeld is proof that women can 100 percent be leaders! Sure, there will be issues female leaders face, but Danielle hopes women won't count themselves out before trying. Danielle recounts a story where a female she was mentoring had the opportunity to take on a new role where significant travel would be required. It was an amazing opportunity with a great path for career growth. However, the woman told Danielle that she was reluctant to take the position because of the travel. She worried how that travel might affect her family.

What's interesting is that the woman didn't even have a family yet. She wasn't married, and she didn't have kids. She was taking herself out of the running for a job because of a future she didn't yet have. Long story short, the woman accepted the job opportunity, met her future husband while traveling, and now has a family and a successful career.

So what does being the vice president and chief technology officer of GE Renewable Energy mean? It means leading a company of tens of thousands of talented individuals while helping change what energy looks like in the future. According to Danielle, we are right now in the energy transition, which is the shift from the global use of fossil-based fuels like coal, natural gas, and oil to renewable energy sources like wind, hydro, and solar. GE Renewable Energy is working on cutting-edge technology to reduce the cost of renewable energy solutions and maintain leadership in this market. Right now, they are making the largest offshore wind turbines in the world. The Haliade-X is taller than many skyscrapers, and each blade is longer than a football field. But just because companies have made great progress with renewable energy doesn't mean they should stop working hard to find new ways to utilize and improve it. Renewable energy is what will enable our carbon-free energy future and energy companies are working to ensure this happens as quickly and cost-effectively as possible.

Can You 3D-Print Something the Size of a Football Field?

You may have seen wind turbines off in the distance on top of mountains or while driving through open areas. From far away, they look huge! But how big can a wind turbine be? The answer is changing, and renewable energy companies are at the cusp of that change.

The idea of 3D printing has been around for a while, starting in the 1950s when a science fiction short story first introduced the concept, but it wasn't really until the 1990s that it became mainstream. Small shapes and figures could be 3D-printed on expensive printers using plastics and metals. But as technology advanced, developers began considering possibilities for 3D printing, with uses in medical fields, manufacturing processes, and even food design, including a 3D-printed chocolate castle. 3D printing started out small in scale, using mostly polymers such as plastics, but as technology continued to develop, so did the possibilities of materials and sizes of 3D-printed objects.

A wind turbine has historically been limited to a height of 100 meters. This was largely because of the enormous concrete base required to support the structure. The blade length of the turbines is also limited by transportation issues. Finding driving routes for larger and larger blades is problematic, and even with current length of blades, only the most skilled of truck drivers are able to handle the job.

But the bigger the turbine, the more renewable energy it can produce. That's where the future gets exciting.

Manufacturing on-site the various parts of wind turbines or transporting them in pieces would reduce logistics issues. If the concrete bases could be larger, they could support a taller tower reaching altitudes with higher wind speeds. And if the blades had a greater reach, more wind could be captured and converted to energy.

Companies like GE Renewable Energy are developing 3D-printing technology on a massive scale, printing concrete towers directly where they will operate. And new materials used to print blades allow for the blades to be not only longer but also 100 percent recyclable, creating a greener future.

There are technical challenges with renewable energy. Renewable plants experience changing dynamics, nonlinearities, and uncertainties as they work to harness natural resources over a system life of 20 to 80 years. The industry is enabled by rapid advances in technology, and Danielle works on ways to ensure that our energy systems are resilient and safe as well as affordable. Wind and solar energy are already lower cost and more efficient than fossil fuel–based power generation today because of the work in system design and development that companies like GE have pioneered.

Further, there are societal challenges with renewable energy, such as the acceptance of wind farms or solar systems in communities across the country. However, these, too, are being addressed in part because renewable energy creates a lot of great-paying jobs while reducing the negative health impacts from burning fossil fuel for energy. The top two fastest-growing jobs in the US are solar installer and wind turbine technician.

Solar Panel Installation

The idea of changing the source of energy for your home sounds like a pretty big process. But what actually happens when you decide to get solar panels installed at your home?

The first big thing to consider is where the solar panels will go. Which side of the roof will face the sun longest? What is the slope of the roof? Is the roof large enough and strong enough to support the number of solar panels needed to generate the electricity your home uses? It's a really good idea to get your roof inspected before installation to make sure it's going to be able to hold the solar panels safely. Professional solar panel installers will be able to check these issues and make sure the panels are in the best possible positions. If the solar panels aren't placed correctly, you won't save as much money over time from the installation.

Another big element of installing solar panels is the electrical wiring involved. High-voltage wires must run from the solar panels to the circuit box for your house, not only being able to power your home but also being compatible with the local electrical grid. This is another place where a solar panel installer is very knowledgeable. They'll be able to wire the system properly and make sure it is safe.

So what happens during a power outage? Will your solar panels be able to power your home while no one else in your neighborhood has power? Not necessarily. A standard solar panel system ties into the local electrical grid. When the local grid power goes out, your power goes out too. There are some exceptions to this, though. If you have a setup that allows you to "island"—effectively switching off your connection to the grid to keep those who may be working on the lines safe—you will still have power during daylight hours. Also, if your system happens to have energy storage installed, then you will still have power even when it is dark. Some homeowners decide to install their solar power system completely off-grid, so it doesn't matter if the grid is down. The downside of being off-grid? You are only able to use whatever power you generate and store. If it is not enough for your needs, there is no local grid for you to pull more power from.

And third, GE is working to make renewable energy even more sustainable with a big focus on recycling. Today some parts of wind turbines are not able to be recycled as easily as others. For example, wind turbine blades are made of a composite of glass and resin material, and separating them presents a challenge. However, there is good progress being made. GE has partnered with a recycling company to take back large wind turbine blades at the end of their life to shred them down and use the material as both feedstock and fuel (replacing silica and coal) in cement kiln coprocessing, a process used to make cement. This "greener cement" could then be used to build cement foundations or towers for new wind turbines. Additionally, GE is working to 3D-print wind turbine blade parts made out of 100 percent recyclable material. The true goal here is to have a completely circular economy, where no new resources are needed to provide the energy we rely on.

Can We Be 100 Percent Green?

The idea of cradle-to-cradle is a concept in which no waste is created. The strategy takes reduce-reuse-recycle to its extreme. When part of a process comes to an end, in the cradle-to-cradle philosophy, it is able to be reused in some form to help fuel the start of the process once again. So instead of thinking of products as cradle-to-grave, in which once something reaches the end of its life cycle, it is thrown away, in a cradle-to-cradle strategy, every bit of it is able to be repurposed to start the cycle over again.

This cradle-to-cradle strategy is a goal to achieve a sustainable economy, not just in energy but in all other sectors, such as transportation, industry, and even consumer goods. Also known as a circular economy, it is one in which there is no waste. From the start of the process until the end, everything is continually used as long as possible. Take, for example, the blades of a wind turbine. In the past, these blades could not be recycled. They were cradle-to-grave. But companies like GE Renewable Energy are constantly working to make processes better. They pioneered a concept for collecting and partially recycling these blades. By shredding them, the composite material could be used as the starting material for a "greener" concrete. But that wasn't good enough. They're also looking for a way to make blades out of 100 percent recyclable material that can then be used to create new blades in the future. This is a great example of cradle-to-cradle. The "death" of one blade fuels the "birth" of a new one. The more the system can be recycled or reused, the closer we get to a circular economy in renewable energy.

The next time an opportunity presents itself to you, before counting yourself out of the race, consider it. Better yet, act upon it. Much of the time, there is nothing to lose by trying. In addition, don't wait for opportunity to come knocking on your door. What inspired action can you take that could change your life for the better? Even when these actions feel out of character, have the courage to take them. They could change your future. They did for Danielle Merfeld.

Danielle Merfeld continues to lead GE Renewable Energy as vice president and chief technology officer in the effort to make renewable energy reliable, affordable, and the new standard. In her spare time, she spends time with her family and dog, hiking, exploring parks, and trying out new food trucks.

Meredith Westafer:
It's Great to Be You

If someone gave you a blank piece of paper and a pencil, could you design a factory? That's the question Meredith Westafer asks potential candidates when she's interviewing them for new positions at Tesla. It's not just a fun exercise. It's the way companies that are on the edge of innovation think. They started by throwing away everything and completely starting fresh. No constraints. No confines of how things have always been done. And when you start approaching problem solving in this way, it changes the way you think—not just in a job, but in your everyday life. Why do things have to be done a certain way? Who makes the rules? And why can't we change them? This is how Meredith Westafer, industrial engineering manager at Tesla, lives her life.

Meredith always figured she'd be an engineer. Not only did she love math; she was great at it. So good, in fact, that in middle school she was placed with a group of other students in an advanced math program. The group of students was encouraged to do well both by teachers and by each other. They had a community, and when you're part of a community like that, it's a great thing. It's empowering and helps reinforce the idea that you can do anything you want.

After graduating high school, Meredith headed to the University of South Florida and enrolled in engineering. That's a pretty broad major, but Meredith wasn't sure what type of engineering interested her the most. She tried an electrical engineering class but determined that wasn't really for her. The same was true for other types of engineering . . . until she found industrial engineering. Meredith realized that industrial engineers weren't concerned with just one single equation. It was the entire system of equations that mattered, and that's what Meredith loved.

After graduating with her master's degree in engineering management and after getting married, Meredith and her husband moved to a small town in South Carolina. He was doing his medical residency there, so Meredith found a job at a small manufacturing plant nearby and got to work. According to Meredith, the job was fine, but as the only female engineer, there were many boundaries Meredith needed to push. Though this turned out to be challenging, it was also a great experience. Meredith learned to make her own path, and she was given the opportunity to try what she wanted as long as she put out good work.

But a trip to San Francisco for a training session changed everything for Meredith. She'd never been to San Francisco, so she decided to explore a bit. One thing that interested her was getting a tour of the new Tesla factory. She checked their website to get information, and hours later, after going down a rabbit hole on the website, found herself not only looking at jobs but also realizing that she had the relevant experience to apply for them. She polished up her résumé and applied, not expecting to hear anything back. But a week later, Meredith received a job offer. It was exciting, but it was a big risk. Tesla was a new company with new technology. They were spending a lot of money but not making any in return. In addition, she would be moving across the country while her husband stayed in South Carolina. But it was also an opportunity Meredith did not want to let pass her by. Her husband supported her completely, and everything just seemed to click into place from there. In what some may consider a selfish move, Meredith took the job and never looked back.

Long-Distance Relationships

Meredith Westafer and her husband lived across the country from each other for two years. She had a great job at Tesla, and he was finishing his medical residency. When you live 2,000 miles away from someone, you can't see each other easily every weekend, but that doesn't mean that the relationship is bound to fail. With work from both partners, long-distance relationships can thrive.

Communication is one of the most important things in any relationship, and all the more so in long-distance ones. Make sure there are clear plans for how often you two will visit, talk, and check in. One partner may feel a single text message every day is sufficient, while the other may expect at least a short phone call. If you talk ahead of time about expectations, there's less chance for disappointment and more chance for success. In addition, even if you can't be there in person for your partner, you can still offer emotional support. Being available, even across thousands of miles, will help each partner know they are not alone.

When you can't be together in person, you can still share many experiences. You both could read the same book or start learning a language. You can set up video chat "date nights," complete with dinner and conversation cards. You can make it a priority to ask about each other's days.

If you truly believe the relationship is worth nurturing and saving, then like everything in life, having a good plan for how to make it last is the most important step you can take. Make your plan. Agree to it. And let your love and life grow.

Meredith started at Tesla as a senior industrial engineer and is now the industrial engineering manager leading the design of new factories. Yes, this means that Meredith no longer gets to do as much of the technical work as she would like, but she can influence the design of many engineers to have a greater impact on the overall project. As a manager, she can't engage in every technical detail, but she can understand them and provide guidance for her engineers to solve problems more efficiently. She has to trust in others to do the technical work, and they in turn have to trust her to lead the team successfully.

A lot of Meredith's job involves working with teams around the world. There are factories in Germany, China, Texas, Nevada, and California. The more factories there are, the more information there is to keep straight. Time lines have to be coordinated. Projects have to be managed. It's a lot to do. But Meredith prides herself on having a team with a solid work-life balance. Not only is this balance important; it allows her and her team to stay motivated and engaged, and in essence allows them to be more successful in all areas of their lives.

Going on a Factory Tour

If you get a chance to visit some place new, walking around to check out the local scene s fun, but a factory tour can really leave a lasting impression on your life. Tesla is just one example of a cool factory tour, but there are so many others. If you're ever in York, Pennsylvania, you can tour the Harley-Davidson factory. In Fairfield, California, a Jelly Belly tour may even come with tasty samples. You can visit a Crayola factory in five different locations, including Orlando, Florida. If you tour the Intel Museum in Santa Clara, California, you'll be able to get a peek inside a cleanroom to see how semiconductors are made. If you want to feel more like you're in *Charlie and the Chocolate Factory*, take a tour of the Hershey's factory in Hershey, Pennsylvania. Maybe music is more your thing? If so, visit the Gibson guitar factory in Memphis, Tennessee. If sweets aren't your thing (not even Ben & Jerry's in Vermont?), then maybe a tour of the Tabasco hot sauce factory in Avery Island, Louisiana, would satisfy your palate. Whatever it is and wherever you go, factory tours are just cool! The list of possibilities could go on and on, and there are places everywhere to visit. So do your research. Check the Internet ahead of time. And make a suggestion to your family. You can turn a boring day into an amazing excursion that the whole family will remember.

Meredith has reached the point in her job at Tesla where being a female leader no longer holds her back, but she does note that her career path was not without its challenges. As a woman and a leader, you often feel like you have to do everything right. You have to be twice as much, all the time. And you have to remind people of your qualifications. All.

The. Time. This can be tricky. Meredith notes that people unwittingly say sexist stuff without even realizing it. Meredith does not sit there and listen. She calls them out on it. She notes that the turning point in her career was when she realized that it wasn't important to be the stereotypical stoic engineer, she could just be herself—lighthearted, quick to laugh, and ferociously analytical. By being herself, everything else fell into place.

Tesla as a company is really about the holistic picture of designing a sustainable future with green energy. Electric cars are a big piece of the puzzle, but if they are plugged into an outlet that pulls energy from a nearby fossil fuel plant, that only solves part of the problem. Tesla is innovating solar products to collect energy, batteries to store that energy for when it's needed, and a variety of electric vehicles to replace fossil fuel-consuming fleets. Electric vehicles are now the next big thing, which has been a huge shift in the time Meredith has been at Tesla. But a lot of building a better, sustainable future is thinking about the whole system and all the many variations, from sports cars and solar panels to semitrucks and massive battery farms. It all has to work together.

This means the manufacturing is getting more exciting each day. And for Meredith, it's an intoxicating environment for an engineer to be at. We are at the edge of a huge shift in how people view electric vehicles, and Tesla is leading the charge both in its product design and its factory design. Not only is the technology cool, but it's also good. Meredith and her teams are doing real work for the betterment of humanity. Also, the products are pretty cool.

So how do companies like Tesla get more electric vehicles on the road? They need everyone's help. There need to be even more super-fast charging networks being installed. More companies need to jump on board. That's the whole point. Everyone needs to do it.

Charging Stations

Can you drive an electric car across the country? You sure can! The most important thing you'll need (besides snacks for the road along with a fantastic audiobook) is a good plan. You may not need to stop for gas every 250 miles, but you will need to stop to charge your car. A charging station is called an EV charger or electric vehicle supply equipment, and their purpose is to supply electrical power for electric vehicles. Most charging stations have a variety of connectors that make them able to be used by all sorts of brands and types of electric vehicles, including hybrids, trucks, buses, and more. These charging stations are often found in public areas like strip malls, grocery store parking lots, and government facilities. Since they're compatible with so many different vehicles, chances are good if you have an electric vehicle, a standard charging station will work for you, but it's important to know what type of connector you have and do your research ahead of time. For example, Tesla uses a proprietary charging port, so if your family owns a Tesla, it may be a good idea to stop at one of their supercharger stations instead of a generic one that may not work.

Major cities generally have plenty of options when it comes to car charging, but what happens when you get to the middle of nowhere? It can definitely add complications to the trip, but it's also not impossible. There are around 45,000 charging stations in the United States, and in as little as 15 minutes, your car can get charged enough for the next 200 miles or so. If you think about it, this is about the same time stopping to fill up your gas tank on a road trip takes (between the bathroom break and grabbing your favorite candy bar).

Before your trip, you can easily see online all the stations where you can stop and charge, and when you're driving, there are various EV charging station apps you can download for use. For many of these, simply put in your destination, and the app will figure out when and where you need to stop. Are you planning on driving from Texas to Washington, DC? That's about 18 stops you'll have to make. That might be a bit more time than what you'd spend in a gas-powered car (it would be about 34 hours in an electric car instead of 24 hours in a gas-powered car), but you'll also save a few hundred dollars on gas. What about a shorter trip, for example, from DC to central Pennsylvania? That requires only one stop for a five-minute charge, so your normal four-hour trip would still take about the same. What if you decide to drive from one corner of the United States to the other, say from Forks, Washington, to Key West, Florida? This trip would take about 55 hours in a gas-powered car. In an electric vehicle you'd be looking at about 79 hours and a gas savings of almost $600.

As for Meredith's main message? It comes from what she's learned. Women are just as capable of doing all the technical things that men are. Everyone has different skill sets, so it's really important to know where you excel. And the more you recognize this, the more it becomes a strength. It's great to be you. It's great to let your personality lead you through your professional career. What makes Meredith an excellent engineer is that she has learned to be herself and to do things her way.

When Meredith Westafer is not leading factory design teams at Tesla, she loves spending time with her husband and two children, horseback riding, skiing, hiking, cooking, and reading as much fiction as possible.

Kara Sprague:
Pivot

Why do so many women shun careers in math and science? According to Kara Sprague, an executive vice president and general manager at F5, technology is the future, and if women want to be part of that future, they need to claim their space in the careers that dominate that field. She believes part of the answer for why women gravitate away from these careers can be found back in the 1980s. Anyone who's watched *Stranger Things* may have an image of what the '80s looked like. Ice cream parlors, shopping malls, video arcades, and ... nerdy boys typing away on home computers tucked away in basements. It's from this image that the stereotype of the lone hacker was born. Before then, there was actually a positive trend of females in tech. Movies like *Hidden Figures* highlight the role women played in the 1960s as programmers for the large mainframe computers many corporations were adopting. But with the transition to personal computers and the rise of the stereotype of the lone hacker in the basement, programming carried a far more negative stigma for young women, and their numbers in the field dwindled. Reversing this trend is part of the work Kara Sprague, a board member of Girls Who Code, strives to accomplish.

Girls Who Code

Girls Who Code was founded in 2012 by Reshma Saujani and is a nonprofit organization that aims to give computer science skills to young women with the hopes of increasing the number of females in STEM. There is a huge difference in the number of females versus males in computer science, but Girls Who Code wants to change that. They run coding programs throughout the school year, teaching topics like programming, robotics, and web design to predominantly middle school and high school girls; there are currently thousands of Girls Who Code clubs across America.

An important part of the Girls Who Code outreach is servicing students that come from historically underrepresented groups. At least 50 percent of the students in the programs include underrepresented minorities, including Black, Latinx, and low-income households. The nonprofit wants to serve all girls, not just those that have ample opportunity. In addition, Girls Who Code had a rapid response to COVID-19, launching a free two-week virtual summer immersion program to address students' needs.

Girls Who Code has expanded to all 50 states and has a global presence in other countries including Canada, the United Kingdom, and India. They have also partnered with a publisher to launch a 13-book series.

Are they successful in their mission? A 2014 study showed that of the 3,000 students who had completed a Girls Who Code program, 95 percent of them went on to study computer science in college. As of 2021 Girls Who Code has over 80,000 college-aged alumni who are entering the workforce, and its programs have served over 300,000 girls since 2012. I'd call that success!

Kara Sprague, now the executive vice president and general manager at F5, was not set on being an engineer from an early age. While she was exposed to programming by age 10, learning to make fractals with BASIC, and thrived in a computer science class in high school, her plans were to study political science at a liberal arts university and later pursue a career in law. That was before she got into MIT. This was right around the time of the dot-com bubble. People were making a lot of money at Internet start-up companies, and everyone wanted to get into computer science. At MIT alone, in Kara's class, a third of the students ended up majoring in computer science and electrical engineering. Kara found herself surrounded by it, and the energy and excitement was visceral. She enrolled in the introduction to computer science courses and discovered she loved programming. She found that when you see many others around you doing something, it's easier to see yourself doing the same.

But college was not without its challenges for Kara. The thing about MIT is that it's filled with students who were valedictorians in their high schools back home, bright young minds used to being the very smartest and best. For many of these students, the course work at MIT, combined with the other learning curves associated with going to college, can be difficult to acclimate to. Because the level and expectations are so much higher, MIT has a pass-fail policy for its freshman year. Kara, like many of her MIT peers, had entered college with a straight-A record from high school and was confident she could handle the workload. She signed up for many courses—far too many courses—and ended up getting a D in her second term. This was a huge wake-up call. She found that she needed to pause and change her approach to studies. Kara learned that the growth and learning she got out of her classes was exactly equal to the work she was putting in. The MIT course work was much more difficult than high school for her. If she was going to do well, her focus needed to be on her studies.

The change in focus worked. At some point at MIT, Kara developed a confidence in herself that she could understand anything as long as she put in the work and spent enough time trying to understand it. Within five years, she graduated from MIT with both her bachelor's and master's degrees in electrical engineering and computer science.

Pass-Fail Freshman Year

Kara Sprague felt prepared for MIT. After all, in high school, she'd been top of the class. But like she learned, MIT is filled with students who were top of their class. And the curriculum was challenging. Kara received a D in one of her classes, but thanks to a policy at MIT, it didn't count against her. MIT has a policy for freshman where the year is pass-fail. There are no grades, which helps students adjust to the challenging environment. There are a handful of other colleges with the same policy, including Brown University, California Institute of Technology, Johns Hopkins University, and Swarthmore College.

If you don't plan to go to one of these colleges, don't panic or think that things aren't fair. Other colleges have programs in place to help freshmen adjust to the huge change. There is generally a fixed time when a course can be dropped by a student for whatever reason, but some colleges allow for late withdrawal from a class. It's not a given, and there must generally be a good reason for dropping the class, so it's always better to withdraw before the deadline to avoid issues. Otherwise, if a class is failed, there are a variety of programs offered by colleges with widely varying restrictions and requirements for dealing with the failing grade. Look into the specific college and read the fine print to know what is possible. Colleges want their students to be successful, so they do try to help to some degree. However, responsibility ultimately comes down to the student to know the policies, not let deadlines slip, and above else, study and work hard.

Summers during college, Kara got internships, working hard to build her skills. And when she graduated, she landed a great job doing hands-on software engineering work as a speech application engineer. She enjoyed her work, but it also left her feeling understimulated and missing the bigger picture. In addition, both working in a cubicle and being the only woman on the team was isolating. She decided to make a pivot in her career trajectory by returning to school and enrolled in the technology and public policy master's program offered by MIT. When she graduated two years later, she went to work for the consulting firm McKinsey & Company, where she was able to put her technical skill to use as a business consultant. This is where Kara found her true passion in leading teams to solve difficult, high-impact problems. She met with clients, researched trends, and identified opportunities in their product and technology strategy. Kara found she loved meeting with clients, learning from their experiences, finding out what inspired or challenged them, and identifying solutions to their toughest problems.

But meeting with so many new clients on such a regular basis turned out to not be without challenges for a female leader. Women in leadership many times may experience prejudice and feel pressure to establish their credibility when meeting new people. Kara was meeting new clients all the time, and with each new client she worked with in consulting, she felt she had to reestablish her credibility. It shouldn't have to be this way. This need is something that can be changed as companies hire more high-level female talent who can be role models, like Kara Sprague.

The consulting firm where Kara worked was already involved in diversity efforts. They were especially focused on attracting and retaining more women. While working there, Kara was presented with an amazing opportunity. The nonprofit organization Girls Who Code reached out to one of Kara's colleagues, asking if the consulting firm might be interested in helping with strategic support. Kara, who was passionate about helping more girls get involved in STEM fields, volunteered to lead the team. Girls Who Code was one of the fastest-growing nonprofits in history, in terms of the speed at which they were able to build charitable momentum toward what they were trying to do, and Kara was eager to support the organization's mission.

Kara herself was very inspired by Reshma Saujani, founder of Girls Who Code, and by the other women on the board. They were role models for her and for her career goals. After a number of years working *with* the board of Girls Who Code, Kara was eventually invited to *join* the board. She has been on the board for several years and is very proud of the impact the organization is having on gender parity in tech. Society needs to do better at every level to encourage more girls to consider STEM careers. Companies need to focus not just on diversity but also on inclusion. Girls need to feel like they belong. And just like computer science at MIT during the dot-com boom, when you see many others like you doing something, it's easier to see yourself doing the same.

Reshma Saujani, Brave, Not Perfect

Reshma Saujani, founder of Girls Who Code, believes that girls are raised to be "perfect" not "brave," but she is on a mission to change this. Before founding Girls Who Code, when she was 33-years-old, Reshma ran for Congress, becoming the first Indian American woman to do so. Yes, she lost (by a big margin, only getting 19 percent of the vote), but according to her this was the first truly brave thing she had done in her life. The experience helped launch her into her true passion of changing how girls are socialized. Girls are taught to smile pretty, to be perfect, to play it safe. Boys, on the other hand, are taught to play rough, climb high, and take risks, learning from an early age how to fail and rebound. Reshma's studies found that even though many times girls outperformed boys, they were more likely to give up upon failure. Boys, upon failing, would redouble their efforts, while girls would convince themselves they were simply not good enough.

While Reshma was on the campaign trail, she visited many schools and saw the huge difference in the number of girls versus boys who were involved in coding. She realized that the issue stemmed from how girls were raised. Women, she noticed, gravitated toward careers they knew they would be great at. They minimized their chances of failure, and what this showed was a bravery deficit.

Girls need to learn to take more risks, even when there is a chance of messing up. It's OK for girls to not be perfect. For any country to grow and be on the leading edge of innovation, half the population cannot be left behind. And it was this realization that spurred Reshma to found Girls Who Code. Too often girls feel like they struggle alone. There must be a sisterhood that lets girls know they are not alone.

Reshma gave a TED Talk in 2016, encouraging girls to step forward and recognize that they must defy their socialization and learn to risk failure. She followed her talk by authoring the book *Brave, Not Perfect: Fear Less, Fail More, and Live Bolder*.

Reshma considers herself a recovering perfectionist and wants the same for other girls. It's OK to take the risk and fail, rather than being stuck, tired, and never getting ahead. With her work, she hopes to rewire toxic patterns that hold women back, and instead wants them to move forward into brave, bold lives.

As for what Kara Sprague enjoys when she's not working through her structured days of workouts, meetings, and problem solving: she loves getting outdoors. Whether it's national parks, skiing, snowshoeing, hiking, or martial arts (she's a third-degree black belt in Taekwondo), Kara is not going to let the world pass her by. She has claimed her spot in it, and through grit and resilience, she has become a leader, a role model, and an advocate. Kara would love to encourage girls to do the same. Technology is the future. Don't let the wave of technology pass you by. Claim your spot in it and don't be afraid to break down biases and have your voice heard.

Part IV
Hackers and AI

Parisa Tabriz: Princess Power

Though not truly royalty, Parisa Tabriz refers to herself as a princess. That's right. Her self-declared title is "browser boss and security princess," and she wants to break down the image of what the stereotypical "princess" is capable of. Parisa believes princesses can do anything. Princesses can be leaders. Princesses can be programmers. Princesses can be computer security experts who are also the head of Google Chrome, just like her. No, her job titles aren't standard. But then again, nothing about Parisa is standard.

Early in Parisa's career at Google, she was set to attend an industry conference in Tokyo. She needed business cards, but all the standard job titles felt too plain for her. With her sometimes pink and red hair, Parisa didn't mind standing out, so she came up with the job title "Security Princess." It started as a bit of a joke, but it stuck. And it made for a nice icebreaker, something that is great when meeting new people. Also, it was a great reminder that you can do serious work without taking yourself too seriously.

The Importance of Business Cards

With everything going electronic these days, do real-life paper business cards really matter? Definitely! Business cards are something that can be given on the spot in person. They can be handed out at trade shows and conferences, easily collected by those passing by. They can give a brief summary of what you do and showcase your abilities. They can show off your brand and your personality. A business card is a quick way to convey lots of information with a personal touch. They make a first impression even when you can't.

Etiquette around business cards is especially important in many cultures. For example, in Hong Kong, when someone presents you with a business card, it is proper to offer them one in return. Don't have one? That could have just cost you a job or an important business deal. In Japan, exchanging business cards is so important, there is even a word for it: *meishi*. Your business card should be held in your right hand, by the corner, so no logos or information is blocked. It should be offered with a bow. And one thing you do not want to skimp on is quality. The quality of your business card reflects the quality of yourself and your company. Make sure your cards are printed on premium paper with an exquisite design. And when you're given a card in return, don't simply shove it in your pocket. It's proper to inspect it and to appreciate it. Don't scribble information on the back. Don't fold it in half to fit it in your wallet. Treat it with respect. It has been given to you as a gift, and you should show your gratitude.

Whatever title you chose to put on your business card (sorry, Security Princess is already taken!), make your card professional, unique to you, and something you are proud to share. This is your moment. If you could be represented by a card, what would it look like?

Growing up with a family who worked in healthcare, college was never a question for Parisa. Her dad, of Iranian descent, was a doctor, and her mom, of Polish American descent, was a nurse. But healthcare wasn't where Parisa's interest lay. She loved computers, and when she started at the University of Illinois in the computer engineering program, she finally got her own computer along with high-speed Internet. Parisa had always loved making and creating things, and she soon taught herself the basics of web design. A couple of the websites she designed got hacked, so she decided to join the computer security club. A couple of internships later, and after graduating with a bachelor's and master's degree in computer science from University of Illinois at Urbana-Champaign, Parisa decided to join Google full-time to work on security.

At Google, Parisa Tabriz is the head of Google Chrome where she manages over 500 people at multiple sites across the world working on the Chrome browser. One of the biggest questions Parisa asks each day is "How do I set up large teams for success? How can I give direction and support without getting in the way?" As a leader of that many people, it's impossible for Parisa to do all the work by herself (and she wouldn't want to!). She provides guidance and pushes power and decision-making down to teams and the people closest to the work.

Keeping Google Chrome safe is no small job, and even with all the work that has gone into it, there are still improvements to be made and bugs to be fixed. Parisa considers Chrome a living and ever-evolving product. The pandemic pushed the boundaries of what was possible with videoconferencing, but it also brought new scams and threats to users online. Parisa and her team want to keep people safe online, and it's a job that never ends as attackers evolve their tactics.

How do you find bugs in Google Chrome? Well, one way is to enlist the help of hackers. Each year at the International Conference on Cybersecurity and Hacking in Tokyo, there is a contest called Pwn2Own. In the contest, a bunch of hackers will try to compromise a computer. They'll try to "pwn" it. If they are successful, they get to keep the computer for free. Some years in the contest, nobody was able to hack Chrome. Other years, bugs are uncovered. When this happens, Parisa and her teams go into high-speed mode to fix them. They hold a 24-hour virtual War Room where they work together to fix the bugs as quickly as possible. Sometimes it's like a gunshot wound. There may not be a comprehensive fix, and instead the bug just gets a couple stitches to hold it over until a real fix can be made.

Hackers

As with coding, the world of hacking has historically been thought of as a male-dominated world. Media has made attempts to change this perception. Back in 1995 the movie *Hackers* came out. Though it didn't get the best ratings on Rotten Tomatoes, it still became a bit of a cult classic. It was about a group of roller-blading high school hackers determined to bring down the patriarchy and featured quotable lines like "Hack the planet" and "Mess with the best, die like the rest." Featured in the movie is a young Angelina Jolie playing the role of amazingly cool female hacker Acid Burn. Every nerdy girl who saw the movie back then wanted to be her. She was smart and cool and lived the secret life all tech females wanted to live. If you watch the movie, keep in mind the Internet was in its infancy back then. It's come a long way, and so has hacking. So, what about female hackers in real life?

Hackers have great skills, and they don't always use them for evil. Take Ying Cracker, for example, a Chinese hacker from Shanghai. Ying uses her genius for good, teaching others the basics of hacking and helping corporations protect their data. Other hackers are not quite as upstanding as Ying. Take Kristina Svechinskaya. This Russian hacker has a specialty, called the Zeus trojan horse. Using her skills, Kristina hacked into bank accounts, stealing over $3 million in a matter of months. Or Gigabyte, born Kim Vanvaeck, who is thought to be the sole creator of quite a few well-known viruses that not only hack into computer systems but destroy the data. But to counterbalance that, back on the side of good is hacker Raven Adler, who graduated high school at 14 and college at 18. In addition to being a talented hacker, Raven is an author and speaker who helps corporations better protect their data and sensitive information.

Why do people get into hacking? There are a variety of reasons. Take Adeanna Cooke, for example. This model, who was often featured in *Playboy*, had private photos stolen and posted on the Internet by someone she knew. What did she do? She taught herself to hack into the site and forced them to take down her pictures. Adeanna is now known as the "Hacker Fairy" and offers her services to other people who have had their private data leaked to the Internet. Another great example is one of the earliest female hackers, Natasha Grigori. Natasha became famous in the hacking community for her stance against child pornography. She started AntiChildPorn.org, where websites containing child pornography can be anonymously reported and subsequently dealt with.

It may be true that in the case of many bugs, one person uncovered the issue. However, it takes an entire team to fix it properly. A lot of technology is about problem solving, constantly learning, and working with teams of other people. Parisa notes that there is a stereotype of a "lone genius" who saves the day. Historically when we watch movies and TV shows with a security expert, it's an antisocial White guy who lives in the basement and doesn't have any friends, so this is what society ends up thinking a security expert is like. This is just not reality! Parisa has done consulting work with entertainment writers to bring a more diverse lens to how they portray STEM experts. She would love to see roles like this evolve more. After all, princesses can be security experts, too.

Moving forward in a career to the point where Parisa is now head of Google Chrome was not a straight path. There was one time at Google where Parisa felt she was doing a good job but felt stuck. She'd hit a point where she wanted to learn more and try new challenges, but her manager didn't share this same vision for her. It was a hard decision to make, but Parisa left the team. She loved the work and the people, but she realized that you can't change everything. At the time, she was not going to be able to influence the kind of change she needed or wanted, so she moved on to a new role that would offer new challenges. As hard as it was to leave a team she loved, this ended up being a great experience in hindsight. These are the kinds of changes that can make or break a career.

Safe Internet Practices

It's great to know that Google is hard at work keeping us safe from bugs in our software. But what kind of bug have we been saved from? One of the biggest bugs that threatens us is what's known as a "zero-day attack." This is when hackers discover a vulnerability in a piece of software and initiate a malware attack through that vulnerability before developers have time to fix it. Not only are single users at risk during this time of attack; large corporations are especially vulnerable. Hackers will use the malware to gain access to customer information including personal and financial data. Because these vulnerabilities often haven't yet been discovered, hackers are able to do quite a bit of damage before anyone notices their actions.

So, what can you do to protect yourself? First, always make sure your browser is up to date. Parisa recommends Chrome, which automatically updates. Second, take a cautious approach to surfing the web. Always be wary of links and attachments as many hackers will set up bogus sites designed to load your computer with malware. Finally, be vigilant when it comes to updating your passwords. The Colonial Pipeline was held ransom by hackers in 2021 because of an old compromised password that hackers used to gain access to the system. If you get a report that your password has been compromised, change it, and change anywhere else you use that same password. Use strong passwords, use different ones for different sites and store them in a password manager, and use two-factor authentication. Keep your data safe!

It might not be hard to imagine that when Parisa became head of security at Google Chrome, it was a bit overwhelming. At one point she looked to her manager for direction. He said, "You can have as much scope as you want. You're responsible for security in Chrome. Go figure it out." He didn't tell her what to do. Instead, he gave her permission to not box herself in. To think big. People want to think big and dream big because that's how they can achieve big things.

So, what about being a woman in such a high-profile position? Well, it hasn't come without its share of hiccups. Parisa recalls one performance review she received where her manager gave her "gendered feedback." He told her that she sometimes came off as "aggressive" and could sometimes be perceived as "stubborn." Parisa notes that if a man received this same feedback, he might have been told he was being "direct" and "persistent." One time in a meeting she was told to be nicer and to smile more. This is definitely not something a guy would have been told in the same situation.

So what should you do when you receive feedback like this? According to Parisa, feedback is a gift. Sure, not everyone is a good gift giver, but it is always a gift to know what people are thinking so you can respond with that insight.

Girls are often taught that if they don't have anything nice to say, then they should say nothing at all. But only when we speak our minds can we have open and honest conversations. Girls are also not always encouraged to have a growth mind-set. They tend to be raised thinking that many of their qualities cannot be changed, like they are either good at math or they aren't. But math, just like everything else, is a skill to practice and functions like a muscle you can strengthen and improve with work.

Parisa wants girls to have confidence (even if you have to fake it), to work hard, to work with others, and to ask for help when needed. These are the keys to being successful. Nobody has it all figured out. Success is about learning constantly, and not being afraid to challenge stereotypes. There is no specific mold you have to fit in. Don't be afraid to be a princess, and find the path that works for you.

Natalie Rusk:
Try It and See

When Natalie Rusk took her first computer class in college, she did not imagine that one day she would become an inventor of a programming language herself. Natalie is one of the creators of Scratch—the most popular coding language for kids, which was developed at MIT Media Lab. Each year, millions of kids around the world use Scratch to create and share interactive stories, games, and animations. The goal of Scratch is not just to teach coding to kids, but to provide all children with opportunities to design projects, solve problems, and collaborate with others.

Natalie Rusk, one of the creative minds behind the development of Scratch, had a vision. She wanted to provide more children with the opportunity to learn to use technology to express their creativity. From an early age, she knew she wanted to work for children's rights. Her interests lay not in teaching but in creating environments where children could create and learn. She noticed that she and her younger brother learned so differently, and from then on, she was on a mission for people to respect kids and their unique strengths and interests.

Unlike so many kids today, Natalie had never really interacted with a computer until she went to college. Her experiences before then had been limited to punch cards and flowcharts. Computers were not available in most schools and homes . . . yet. But when Natalie got to college, she enrolled in the introduction to computer science course, and she found that she really liked it. The best part was that for the final project, students were given a choice of making a project. The project was not only a way to show their programming skills, it was a way to create something useful.

But even as engaging as the class was, Natalie was not sold on pursuing a future in computer science. Her professor wore a wizard hat to class, and the graduate students were making a video game featuring their wizard professor. As playful as it might sound, it also made the group (and the field) feel like it was not relevant to her goals and interests. Natalie knew her real purpose was to help people, and despite the growing popularity of the field, she didn't see a real purpose in continuing on with computer science. She wasn't sure how it could fit with her vision of helping children.

Video Games Created by Women

The video game world has historically been dominated by men, but the good news is that things are changing. More and more companies are seeking out talented women with a creative vision. And yes, while many video games have been created and designed by men, there are also some very well-known ones that have been designed by women. If you want to think old-school, one of the most popular Atari games, *Centipede*, had a woman as one of the lead designers. More recently and definitely a classic, *Portal*, the popular puzzle-solving game (where the cake most definitely is a lie), had a woman as the design lead. If you're wondering if any women have worked on first-person shooter RPG games, the answer is definitely yes! Both *BioShock* and *BioShock 2* had a woman as the project lead who later went on to work on *The Walking Dead* (the video game) and *Minecraft* (story mode).

Women have also reenvisioned video games, taking a look at how women are portrayed in games and changing that. Take Lara Croft. When the game first came out, it was all about Lara's sex appeal. But with the 2013 release of *Tomb Raider* and a female writer on the job, Lara Croft became less about the sex appeal and more about a strong protagonist that young girls could look up to as a role model. And as for more recent games, *Animal Crossing: New Leaf* and *Animal Crossing: New Horizons* had a female director who, when she saw the discrepancy in gender, hired a team made up half of females to develop the game, and she encouraged everyone to express their creative ideas.

Women most definitely can and do design video games. If you love designing video games in Scratch, then maybe video game design is a possibility for your future!

Natalie focused on learning other subjects. But something about computer science drew her back, so her senior year, she enrolled in another course. She often got the feeling that people were wondering "Why are you here?" It was a question Natalie also asked herself. Around this time Natalie came across the book *Second Self* by Sherry Turkle. It introduced the idea that computers are not just tools but can provide a way to express ideas and reflect on our social and psychological lives.

Natalie was inspired. She applied to education schools that linked computer science with psychology and education and ended up going to Harvard. While there, she enrolled in a course at MIT with a focus on children and learning and their passions and culture. It was about how computers could support children, their interests, and their voices. It was about creating spaces where kids could take their ideas and make them come to life. Where kids could express themselves with technology. This is where Natalie found her people.

Now, with a master's in education, specializing in interactive technology, Natalie had the opportunity to work on lots of projects. After graduating, Natalie began collaborating in science museums where families create together, which really drew her in. This was something different. Natalie spent a lot of time thinking about how to help people learn about computers and use them for their own ideas.

She also studied how kids handled different situations. Consider programmable Legos. Some kids would build something, and if it fell apart, they would decide they were no good at it and move on. But for other kids, when their Lego projects fell apart, they would work to think up a better idea. They would try something new. What was it about this situation that made kids act differently, and what could Natalie do to leverage that information and turn it into something kids could use? It was from this thinking that Scratch was born.

MIT Media Lab

According to Natalie, working at the MIT Media Lab is her dream job. From the environment to the people, it is across the board filled with fantastic work, ideas, and opportunities. Scratch, which has been used by millions of people worldwide, is just one of many projects that have been developed at the lab. And it's not a place that's just all about computer coding. Technology, media, science, art, and design all come together for the amazing research being done there.

The labs are divided into over twenty groups, including things like Personal Robots, with the mission of "building socially engaging robots and interactive technologies to help people live healthier lives, connect with others, and learn better," Camera Culture, with the mission of "making the invisible visible—inside our bodies, around us, and beyond—for health, work, and connection," Personal Justice, with the mission of "exploring new forms of social justice through art," and Opera of the Future, with the mission of "extending expression, learning, and health through innovations in musical composition, performance, and participation." Those all sound pretty cool, don't they?

Some research projects originally developed in the MIT Media Lab have been spun off to become products or public software of their own, like Lego Mindstorms, the Benton hologram used in most credit cards, Fisher-Price's Symphony Painter, and Taito's Karaoke-on-Demand Machine. In addition, spin-offs of the lab are numerous, including E Ink, the technology used for electronic paper displays in Kindles and Nooks, and Affectiva, which is software that detects emotions in pictures of faces.

It's great to think about scientists, artists, educators, and programmers all working together to create the next generation of projects, and having such an amazing time doing it!

One of the projects that Natalie codeveloped at the Media Lab is the Clubhouse Network, a program that gives kids from underserved communities a safe space to explore new ideas. There are centers where young people create things based on their interests. They would try to program, but the current programming tools were difficult to use. And since there was not an easy entry point, many kids would give up. The question Natalie and her colleagues asked was whether there was a way they could easily create their own animations and make their own games.

The problem with pitching the idea of coding to kids was that there was this idea that coding was hard. And yes, certain aspects of coding can be challenging. What Natalie and her colleagues envisioned was not only a visual interface but a new language. They pitched the idea and received a National Science Foundation grant to work on the project. Scratch was born.

Once developed, the great thing about Scratch was that it grew in a very grassroots manner. They offered workshops to educators who would then introduce it to their students. Kids would come home and show their parents. It's not just every tool out there that a teacher will introduce to a kid and have the kids be so excited about that they want to go home and work on it.

What really excited Natalie about Scratch is seeing how kids create projects to express their ideas and interests. Kids across the world are having their voices heard through their Scratch projects. Yes, it is learning, but it's not primarily about learning. It is about expressing yourself and your ideas.

And what about mistakes? Natalie influenced the design of Scratch to make sure there are no error messages. Kids try programming something, and maybe what happens isn't what they intended to happen, but something else cool could happen. They could build on that. What's great is that this "try it and see" mentality builds confidence not just in coding but in other areas of kids' lives also.

Gaining Creative Confidence

It's true that Scratch is not the same as Instagram or Snapchat, but that doesn't mean users can't interact. On Instagram, users can have millions of followers. On Scratch, the top users currently have hundreds of thousands of followers. Being top of the Scratch leaderboard may not be something you can monetize. It won't get you sponsorships or make you go viral, but it's still got a lot to recommend it.

Natalie Rusk shared the story of one young girl who went on to study computer science in college. Back in middle school, while taking a coding course, she felt like since she was a girl no one in class really listened to her. She was one of the only, if not the only, girls in class, and she was easily dismissed. People thought she just wasn't that great at programming, and nobody really gave her a chance. But in the online world, things were a bit different.

On the Scratch platform, this girl was respected for her projects and helping others. She'd code up amazing projects and get all sorts of positive encouragement. People got excited when she commented on their projects. They remixed her projects and praised her hard work. And that experience gave her the confidence to continue on with coding. If she'd relied on that confidence from middle school coding class alone, she may have never gone on to pursue STEM and earn her computer science degree. With the confidence of Scratch boosting her, she sought out a community, looking for a school with powerful females in leadership positions, and from there she kept moving forward, finding a place where she could express her ideas and not be dismissed just for being a female.

Wherever it is that you can find your community and express your ideas, seek it out. Refuse to be dismissed. And grow into the person you were meant to be!

The research group where Natalie works is a place where people come in with a smile. There are things everywhere to create with. A giant Lego Scratch cat greets you at the door. Playful sculptures hang from the ceiling. Bins are filled with a colorful combination of craft materials, building bricks, motors, and more. It's a fun, creative environment. A community of staff and students from around the world who care about kids.

Natalie Rusk believes that if you have a great idea, you should pursue it. The real purpose of STEM should be about helping people around the world. You belong in this space, and you can make a difference. And to do this, find the things that you feel aren't quite right the way they are, and make something around it that other people can see. Express your thoughts to others. Don't think that you don't belong here. You do belong here. Maybe things do need to change, and you can be one of the people who makes that change happen.

Sophia Velastegui:
Keep Moving Forward

How does Netflix know what show to suggest to you next? And when you're looking at the home screen and see all your possible choices, are the shows that are advertised to you the same as the shows being advertised to your best friend or parents? Most likely not. The reason: artificial intelligence.

The first thing that pops into many people's minds when they hear the term "artificial intelligence" is science fiction. Movies like *The Terminator* or *Star Wars*, with droids like R2-D2 or C-3PO. But artificial intelligence doesn't just happen in the future after an apocalypse where robots have taken over the world or in some galaxy far, far away. Artificial intelligence is very real right now, and Sophia Velastegui is on the leading edge of it.

AI in Movies

Movies and television shows are known for having some of the best and most memorable artificial intelligence machines. Some of these you may have heard of, and some may be brand new to you. Whether you're into hard science fiction or lean more toward the eccentric, there's bound to be something for you out there.

Back in 1956 Robby the Robot first saved the day in *Forbidden Planet*. The Alien movies have seen a recent gain in popularity with AIs such as the newer David in *Prometheus* and *Covenant* and the more classic Bishop in *Aliens*. *Star Trek* has Data, an android desperate to get in touch with his human side. *Star Wars* won fans over with the friendship between the two droids R2-D2 and C-3PO (these are not the droids you are looking for). For the newer Star Wars movies, BB-8 wins over the audience's hearts by rolling around to help save the day. (By the way, the name BB-8 comes from "ballbot" and the way the droid looks like the number eight.) The Matrix series made an extremely memorable character with its Agent Smith (and his constant monotone "Mr. Anderson"). *Terminator*, of course, put artificial intelligence on the map for the gym rats, featuring Arnold Schwarzenegger as a cyborg from the future.

Artificial intelligence got in touch with its emotional side with *Edward Scissorhands*, a creation made of plastic, metal, and, yes, scissors (for hands, in case you didn't figure that out). Wall-E, a cleanup robot left on our post-trash-apocalypse planet, solves Rubik's cubes and gives hope back to Earth in the form of a single surviving plant in the 2008 Pixar release. Always a classic, we'd be remiss to not mention *The Iron Giant*, featuring a "giant" robot who crash-lands near Maine and befriends a young boy. The animated movie *Robots* features Rodney Copperbottom, a robot who moves to Robot City hoping for his big break. And of course we can't forget Baymax, the healthcare provider robot in *Big Hero 6* who teaches us the important lesson that we are part of the story.

As for exploring just how far artificial intelligence can go, *Westworld* has an entire cast of AIs, living in the Wild West and discovering their true nature, which is not even known to them. And *Black Mirror* features artificial intelligence concepts in many of its episodes, exploring the vast possibilities of just how much AI can be used for.

Sophia is Microsoft's chief technology officer of AI for Microsoft Dynamics 365, which means she leads the AI strategy for and development of applications that corporations need to run their businesses. Much of her job deals with interfacing to customers. Imagine you own a company. To help run the different functions of the company, whether it be marketing, sales, finance, customer service, or supply chain, you need software's help. Sophia's job is to come up with the right strategies to infuse artificial intelligence into the software for all those functions. With the right artificial intelligence in place, companies can learn more about their customers and their own businesses.

We've all had those moments of calling customer service where we're connected with a person, a virtual agent, or a recorded voice that uses a chain of questions to try to figure out what it is we're looking for, sometimes to our immense frustration. It might seem simple, but the AI in the software has to understand what we are saying and then find out all the information related to the topic we're asking about. The AI uses keywords and then looks up articles or documents to help explain how to solve those problems.

What Is AI?

Artificial intelligence is a term lots of people use these days. Do you know what it means? Let's start with what it doesn't mean. Natural intelligence is intelligence that is displayed by humans or animals. Artificial intelligence is intelligence that is displayed by machines. In the study of artificial intelligence, systems must perceive their environment and take actions that will optimize their chances of success.

Let's look at this in practice. If you load up Netflix and immediately search for the latest anime shows, select one, and watch it, what do you think will happen the next time you turn on Netflix? Well, what is Netflix's goal? The company wants you to watch as many shows as you possibly can. If the AI system is going to be successful in this goal, it needs to recommend shows to you that it thinks you will want to watch. You like anime? How about *Toy Story* next? No! Just because anime and *Toy Story* are both animated does not mean you have a high likelihood of wanting to watch the Pixar movie. Instead, it's going to shuffle through its other anime shows and suggest one of those to you. To take it even further, it's going to check what you've already watched. If you've seen *Seven Deadly Sins* just last week, then maybe recommending that isn't the best choice. In addition, it's going to check the genre of the anime. Was it funny? Sexy? Serious? The AI system will add that to its search parameters and try to come up with recommendations that you aren't going to be able to resist.

The next time your parents complain that you're watching too much Netflix, tell them that it's not your fault. It's the fault of the AI system. If artificial intelligence machines weren't so smart, maybe you wouldn't be able to find anything else to watch.

As to where Sophia thinks artificial intelligence will be in the future, she believes it will seamlessly be a part of everyday life, with us at all times. We're not far from there already when you think about it. We have smartphones with social media apps that give us suggestions for how to respond to our friends, smartwatches that alert us when it's going to rain, and step trackers that remind us when we need to be more active. Our homes are decked out with learning thermostats that change the temperature the closer we are to home, doorbells that record package deliveries, and virtual assistants that predict when we need to reorder our dog food. And when it comes to entertainment, all we have to do is open Spotify to get recommendations for what music to listen to next. There are real people behind the scenes who make this possible using computer algorithms. Sophia is one of those people.

When Sophia was younger, she didn't dream of being a CTO at Microsoft. She actually wanted to be a ninja. In fact, she and her brother started training for this dream in elementary school. But after a neighbor caught them sneaking across the roof of their house, their ninja aspirations came to an end. All was not lost, however. Sophia's soon developed an interest in STEM, and it started with some hands-on design work. Like many homes, to control the television and electronics, Sophia's home had more remotes than they knew what to do with. There was a remote for the television, the VCR, and the cable box. Sophia took it upon herself to hook them all together to create her own universal remote, which it should be noted her family was not happy about. They didn't appreciate the overall look of duct tape and wires sticking out everywhere and wanted her to put it back the way it was. But she was hooked. She loved figuring out how things could be connected.

Growing up in New York, Sophia told her parents she wanted to attend the Bronx High School of Science. It was a two-hour commute each way and included a quarter-mile walk and three trains. Her parents told her that if she decided to go, she couldn't change her mind. Sophia had no intention of changing her mind. By then, she was determined to be in STEM, and Bronx Science was the best choice for her future. Her parents still weren't so sure.

The path was not without a few bumps in the road. Sophia's family is Korean, and her grandparents were raised on traditional Korean farms. Their priority was making sure their daughter found a husband. They worried that if she went into engineering, she would never find one. In fact, her grandparents strongly recommended she go into pottery instead. No, Sophia did not want to go into pottery—she did not consider herself the least bit artistic—but pushing back against cultural expectations can be hard. Thankfully, a mentor at her church said, "You're the top student at the Bronx Science magnet school, and you're going to graduate a year early. You can do anything you want because you have the talent and grit to achieve it." That gave Sophia the confidence she needed to pursue her passion. Sophia went on to attend college and receive her bachelor's degree from Georgia Tech and her master's degree from UC Berkeley, both in mechanical engineering.

Even after getting her degree in engineering and landing a great job in semiconductors as a mechanical engineer, her parents weren't quite sure what she actually did in her job. In response, Sophia sent them a picture of herself in a clean room, dressed in a white protective coverall suit. Her parents were very impressed. They thought she was an astronaut! (Do a quick search on cleanroom suit, and this misunderstanding might make more sense.) Her parents told the entire Korean community about their "astronaut daughter." Years later, Sophia found out about this mistake at church when the pastor prayed for "Sister Sophia, who is trying to be the first Korean astronaut in space." Oops.

Though Sophia is most definitely *not* an astronaut, her job is challenging and demanding and full of responsibility. But she's still not sure if her parents understand her work to this day.

Twenty Questions

If you've ever played a game of Twenty Questions against a computer, you may have been amazed when the computer guessed your answer correctly. How does it do that? How is it so smart?

One way to implement artificial intelligence in a game like Twenty Questions is using something called a decision tree. For this, imagine there is a starting point. Let's call it a node. You can visualize it as a circle if you want. This is the first question. For this question, there are three possible answers: yes, no, and maybe. For each answer, an arrow is drawn from the initial node. Now, there are three more nodes. For each of these three nodes, there are three possible answers, so each of these nodes will also have three more nodes. If we look at how this can grow into so many answers that the computer can guess what you are thinking, let's look at the total possible number of nodes after twenty questions.

After one question, there are three nodes (this is three to the first power, 3^1). After two questions, there are nine nodes (3^2). After three questions, there are 27 nodes (3^3). After 20 questions, there are 3^{20} possible nodes, or about 3.5 billion answers! The thing you were thinking of is bound to be one of those 3.5 billion answers. The machine uses a decision tree, asking questions for you to answer, and moving in the right direction until it gets to the end. And that is how the machine is able to use artificial intelligence to determine the most likely answer!

In addition to working on artificial intelligence itself as an engineer, Sophia's title, chief technology officer, means she's a leader at Microsoft. She invests 70 percent on her job requirements, 20 percent on coaching, mentoring, and learning, and 10 percent on intentional networking with people in her industry. The ratio may change with career advancement but all three must be an active part of a career plan to maximize someone's full potential. This method has led Sophia to be the cochair at the World Economic Forum and a board director for a public company, Blackline. This is in addition to her responsibilities at Microsoft.

According to Sophia, being a leader as a female and as a minority, people can have certain biases about you, but these biases can be overcome. Sophia encourages others to be true to themselves and to set themselves up for success. It's also important to overcome biases in advance. One great way to do this is to not assume people know who you are or what you do. Make your accomplishments clear ahead of time. Some might consider this "bragging," but it's actually setting the context. Unless you make clear what you have done or how you have advanced, you can't assume anyone will know.

Sophia's path to success has been unique. In any path you take in life, it's important to remember that everyone's style will be different. Sophia does a great job of showing this with an example. She says that it's a lot like rock climbing, something Sophia and her family enjoy. In rock climbing, everyone starts with different advantages. For example, Sophia is 5'4" and her husband is 5'11". This means he can reach a lot farther than she can. They both have the same goal in mind: reach the top. But when it comes time to decide which rock to hold on to as they move forward, they each have to pick the rock that is right for them. Any goal in life is the same way, whether it's getting a college education or becoming a leader. You have to create your own unique path to reach your goal. And even if you don't know exactly what you want to do when you grow up, it helps to choose a direction and move forward. Just like with rock climbing, even if you don't take the straightest path, keep moving up, so each step you take is closer to your goal and a future filled with success.

Sophia Velastegui believes in being unapologetically ambitious. She says to be deliberate in how you move forward to meet your goals. Have a strategy. Do it through intentional risk. Be disciplined. Watching YouTube how-to videos does not make you an expert. Learn through having real experiences. If you screw up, try again as many times as you need to. Remain curious along the journey to expand your knowledge. Schooling is just the beginning. This is a lifelong pursuit.

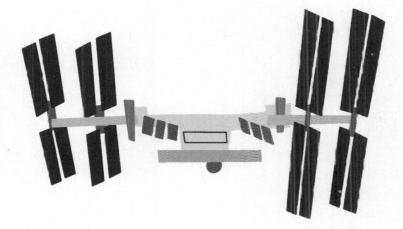

Part V
Rockets and Space

Swati Mohan:
Persevere

Imagine you'd been working on a project for years. But it wasn't just any project. It was a really important project, with an impact that stretched across not just the state or country but the entire solar system. When the moment of truth came, and it came time to determine if the project you'd been working on was going to succeed or fail, the entire world was going to be watching. Watching you. You were going to be the public face of the project.

Would you be nervous? Of course you would! Many people would. What would you do to deal with your nerves and make it through the event without breaking down? Well, you might pretend that it was just one more simulation. That's what Swati Mohan did during the entry, descent, and landing of the Mars

Perseverance rover. She went through the steps one by one, like she had for every practice run thus far. Except this was no practice run. This was the real thing, and Swati Mohan was the public face that was going to be broadcast around the world.

It's known as the seven minutes of terror, and a lot of things have to go right to get Perseverance safely on the surface of Mars. But it was way more than seven minutes that led up to the moment when Swati Mohan announced to the world, "Touchdown confirmed. Perseverance safely on the surface of Mars, ready to begin seeking the signs of past life." It was years of hard work. It was teamwork. It was perseverance.

Approaching Mars

The Seven Minutes of Terror sounds like something from a horror movie. It's a nail-biting-enough experience that this is not far from the truth. After years of preparation for a landing on Mars, everything must go right in the seven minutes of terror, or all can be lost. So, what happens in those seven minutes? Quite a few things, actually.

First, the spacecraft must enter the atmosphere without burning up. This means being at the correct speed and angle for optimal entry, with proper protection from the heat shield. Once this is done, the spacecraft needs to slow down. It enters the atmosphere at 12,500 miles per hour. Deploying the parachute at this speed would be disastrous, so it goes through a series of steps to create drag from the atmosphere. It also needs to steer properly, making sure it's heading in the right direction toward its landing spot. Once it's going in the right direction and has slowed down enough, the parachute is deployed. This should slow the spacecraft down to around 200 miles per hour. That's still too fast to land, but successful deployment of the parachute is a big achievement on the path to a safe landing.

As the spacecraft continues to make its way to the landing spot, it drops its heat shield, jettisons its parachute, and ignites its jetpack. It also has to make sure to evade the parachute. At this point it slows to 1.7 miles per hour. That's almost nothing, but the terror isn't over yet. Cables are then deployed that are used to lower the rover to the surface. Once the rover touches down, these cables are cut. And finally, after touchdown, the jetpack must be flown to a safe distance away where it will crash on the surface.

All that happens in seven minutes, and because of communication delays, none of it can be controlled by humans in real time. Seven minutes of terror? Absolutely!

Swati Mohan always knew college was in her future, but for many years, she was sure that she'd be a pediatrician. Why? That's what she had said when somebody once asked her when she was in the second grade what she wanted to be when she grew up. It was an easy profession to relate to, so that's what she said she wanted to be. She figured since she'd said it (even though she was only in second grade), now she had to follow through. But high school physics and the right teacher changed everything.

In her senior year of high school, Swati had to choose between AP Physics and AP Biology. The courses were only offered at the same time, and unless Swati could figure out a way to duplicate herself, she could only take one. Since watching *Star Trek* at a young age, she'd always loved space. For fun, she'd check out books from the library on planets, how stars formed, the big bang theory, and space travel. With the benefit of a phenomenal physics teacher, physics came easily to Swati. Force equals mass times acceleration. That's all there was to it. Swati realized that one simple formula could explain everything, from balls rolling to planets orbiting. So, AP Physics it was, and then from there, it was on to a degree in aerospace engineering.

But even then, Swati Mohan wasn't sure what to do with her degree. Her undergraduate adviser helped her decide with a series of simple questions that paved the path to the landing of the Mars rover years later.

"Do you like things that stay still? Or do you like things that move?" he asked.

"I guess I like things that move," Swati answered.

"OK, well, do you like things that move slowly or move fast?" he asked next.

"I like things that move fast," Swati said.

And with a few more questions, Swati was placed in the attitude controls group working on building a satellite. Now, years later, she's a guidance, navigation, and control systems engineer at NASA Jet Propulsion Laboratory. Maybe all those career questions counselors ask do have the ability to lead you to the right career!

Why Land on Mars?

What is it about Mars that keeps our interest piqued? Mars is rocky and barren. Its atmosphere is super thin and filled with dust, making it impossible to walk around for humans without a space suit. There are no plants. No animals. If you had to compare it to somewhere on Earth, it's like Antarctica but without the snow. It does have two moons (Phobos and Deimos), unlike Earth, but that's not enough to justify spending billions of dollars to observe from the night sky. So why Mars? Are we trying to move there, like what's been portrayed in science fiction books and movies for years?

Since space exploration began, dozens of spacecraft have visited Mars. We've discovered evidence of water, organics, and methane. By visiting Mars now, scientists are looking for signs of past and current life which would help us discover if life is unique to Earth. If signs of life (ancient or current) are found are Mars, it could show that life may be abundant in our universe. Traveling to and exploring Mars also helps scientists test new technologies, like communicating across vast distances and collaborating with other scientists around the world.

Traveling to Mars can also help scientists understand how humans perform in low gravity and weightless situations and how space radiation affects humans. The knowledge gained here can be used for space travel moving forward, even space tourism. And finally, traveling to Mars also helps satisfy basic human curiosity. Humans often wonder about their place in the universe, and space travel can help us take a step toward understanding the answer.

The week leading up to the landing of Perseverance, everything was going smoothly. Every day Swati and the team knew major things could go wrong. As each day passed without incident, the anxiety level kept ratcheting up. They knew that if something was going to go wrong, it would be much better to have it happen sooner rather than later. Sooner, and there would be time to make adjustments, like minor course corrections. But as the moment of the landing got closer and closer, the window for adjustments continued to shrink. Adjustments can't be made instantly. It takes eleven minutes to transfer a message from the control room to the Perseverance rover. Even up until the morning of the landing, messages were being transmitted to Perseverance. But about an hour and a half before landing, the transmitter was turned off. No more adjustments would be made. Everything had to go right on its own from that point forward.

What were those steps that had to go right? Perseverance had to enter the atmosphere successfully. The parachute had to deploy. The parachute was critical in slowing Perseverance down so it wouldn't crash into the surface of Mars. And then it needed to make sure to land in a safe spot. Each success was a major milestone, but the team was given strict instructions not to celebrate these milestones. Celebration was only allowed after the touchdown call was made. And when Swati Mohan made that touchdown call, the room erupted. Only then, amid the cheering, did Swati finally allow herself to feel the accomplishment. She and the team had done it. The Mars Perseverance rover had successfully landed on the surface of Mars.

Are We Headed to Venus Next?

We've often heard about space travel to Mars, but what about the other planets? Could we be heading to Venus next? Back in 1962, Venus was actually the first planet to be explored by a NASA spacecraft. The Mariner 2 flew by the cloud-covered world, scanning it. In 1989 NASA's Magellan used radar to map the surface of Venus, and there have been others. Soviet spaceships have actually landed on the surface of Venus, but owing to the extreme heat and crushing pressure, they didn't last long.

Now, NASA has its sights set on Venus once again. NASA recently announced two new programs aimed to explore the bright planet. DAVINCI+ (which stands not for the artist-inventor but for Deep Atmosphere Venus Investigation of Noble gases, Chemistry, and Imaging) will study the composition of the atmosphere. It will study how Venus formed and look for the answer to whether Venus ever had an ocean in its past. It will also seek to get high resolution pictures of geological structures on Venus known as tesserae, which can be compared to Earth's continents.

The second mission is known as VERITAS (Venus Emissivity, Radio science, InSAR, Topography, and Spectroscopy), and its primary goal is to map the surface of Venus. The goal is to learn more about Venus's geological history and study when it formed differently than Earth. The mission will examine the types of rocks that make up Venus and seek to learn if there are active volcanos releasing water vapor into the atmosphere.

The good news is that we don't have to wait that long for these exciting missions. The two missions are expected to launch between 2028 and 2030.

So why is something like Perseverance landing on Mars such a big deal? According to Swati, it shows the nation what we are capable of if we work together and embrace the diversity of thought and talent and mind-sets that are required to achieve any complex goal. Perseverance wasn't the work of a single group of engineers at NASA. It was the work of organizations across the country, each building different parts of the rover, and of scientists from around the world. Different people from different backgrounds working together, each critical in achieving success. The Mars rover landing was much greater than the sum of its parts.

The reason Swati Mohan is where she is today is because she was true to herself. She kept her strengths, weaknesses, and passions in mind to create her own unique path (all the way to Mars!). There is no one way to get a spaceship to Mars, and there is no one way to achieve a goal or reach a dream. Just because somebody else accomplished something one way does not mean it's the only way to do it. Each path to success is different, and thinking outside the box and taking the time to plan your path could be the key to making your dreams come true.

Swati encourages others not to try to be someone else. Be true to yourself! Swati Mohan was true to herself. She learned from her experiences, both good and bad, and used them as stepping stones to improve. She worked hard. She didn't give up. And she persevered.

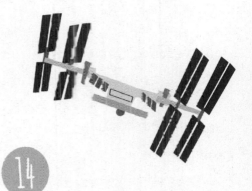

14

Victoria Garcia:
Speak Up

Victoria Garcia, a Cuban American who was born profoundly deaf—meaning she was unable to detect any sound at all—never imagined she would actually work for NASA, her dream job. Sure, she knew she wanted to be an engineer, but NASA felt way out of her reach. Yet one circumstance led to another, and now Vicky not only works for NASA as a systems engineer; she also leads a team of over 20 people on projects like environmental controls and life-support systems that will help explorers venture into deep space.

Vicky Garcia always loved problem solving and fixing things. From an early age, she was appointed the "handyman" around her house, installing ceiling fans or looking up on the brand-new Internet how to do things. She enjoyed math and science—well, except for chemistry, which she considered herself bad at—but engineering isn't just defined by "being good at math and science." It is about problem solving and a passion for figuring out how things work.

As much as Vicky loved engineering, she shied away from communication. In high school, Vicky had a hard time with meetings and groups. She actually still does. Some people understand her deaf accent just fine. Some people don't and claim she speaks too fast, something challenging for Vicky since she tends to get so excited about her work. But thinking forward about a career, the idea of meetings and working as part of a team stressed her out, so she decided to enroll in college as a computer engineering major. She figured there would be less communication in this field and more just sitting in a cubicle working on a computer each day not talking to other people.

Learning to speak up for herself turned out to be the biggest tipping point for Vicky. In college Vicky soon learned that there was no avoiding meetings. Sure, she knew her stuff, and others that she was working with knew this, but Vicky communicates in a way that is different than many deaf people. She reads lips and is only so-so at signing. So, in meetings, if someone turned their back to her, she could not see what they were saying. This went on, with Vicky not saying anything, until one day she finally spoke up. She said, "I'm sorry but you guys are going to have to turn and face me." It was challenging. It was hard. But it was also necessary. And from that point forward, communications were great. So great that Vicky actually changed her major from computer engineering to mechanical engineering. She realized that by speaking up, she could work with teams, and mechanical engineering was where her true passion lay.

But the future for Vicky Garcia was not without more challenges ahead. When Vicky graduated from Rensselaer Polytechnic Institute with her bachelor's degree in mechanical engineering, she began looking for a job. This was way before the time of Zoom calls. Email was around, but it was not the norm yet when applying for jobs. Everything was done by phone interview.

But being deaf, Vicky couldn't simply pick up the phone when it rang and do a job interview. She needed to use a system called TTY. If you aren't familiar with what a TTY phone call might look like for a deaf person, Vicky would type out messages that were then translated and sent to the person on the other end of the phone. When the other person was responding, their response would be typed out for Vicky to read. This resulted in about five to ten second delays for each communication, which might not sound like a lot but can make for some very awkward conversations.

What Is TTY Mode?

A TTY (teletypewriter) is a special device that lets people who are deaf, hard of hearing, or speech impaired use the telephone to communicate by allowing them to type messages back and forth to one another instead of talking and listening. It's not some bulky device. In fact, many cell phones have TTY mode. That said, a TTY device can also be used to interface with a cell phone if TTY mode is not available (though this is a pretty outdated method).

Text messaging, video calls (using both sign language and lip reading), and video relay services (which is a service for those Deaf users who specifically use American Sign Language to communicate with video equipment) have replaced much of the need for TTY services, but when Victoria Garcia was going through her interview process, here are the basics of how it would work: The interviewer would verbally ask a question, which would be transmitted to the TTY service where it would be typed out for Victoria to read. She would then type an answer in response, which would be transmitted and then vocalized for the interviewer to hear. It's easy to see how this back and forth could cause a delay.

TTY is a standard used for those who are deaf, but other services exist for those with other disabilities who wish to communicate with a person using a standard telephone, including TeleBraille, which allows a DeafBlind caller to receive their conversation at a slower pace, and Spanish to English, which allows a Spanish-speaking caller to receive their conversation in Spanish.

Vicky applied for about 20 positions. She got maybe five calls back, and for each of those calls, she then had to explain the TTY situation. Of those five callbacks, only one person brought Vicky in for an in-person interview. According to Vicky, it went badly. While reading lips, she misunderstood a single word (Vicky interpreted the word to be "cast" instead of "CAD"), which led her to talk about the wrong subject at length. The interviewer, not wanting to appear rude, did not correct her. Needless to say, Vicky did not get the job.

It was around that point that Vicky learned about a program called Entry Point! that helps connect STEM candidates with disabilities to the right employers. But Vicky didn't want to get a job just because she was deaf. She felt her qualifications should speak enough for her. Yet her only in-person interview drove home the point that she had extra challenges to overcome, so she signed on with Entry Point! Entry Point! works with many amazing companies, including NASA. When Vicky got an internship at NASA, she felt like it was her dream opportunity. Yes, she still had to prove herself, but her foot was in the door. And since that time, Vicky has never left. She had always felt like NASA was way beyond her hopes, and yet not only is Vicky now working for NASA, she is excelling.

What Is Entry Point!?

Entry Point! is a signature program of the AAAS (American Association for the Advancement of Science) Project on Science, Technology and Disability, and it was also critical in helping Victoria Garcia find a job she was qualified for. The main goal of the program is to discover new talent and increase diversity by helping undergraduate and graduate students with disabilities get into STEM fields. The program won't give you a job—candidates need the technical skills and knowledge that Entry Point! partners are looking for—but it will help give you a chance to get noticed. The reason they do this? Diverse perspectives and lifestyles will help broaden the creative culture of many companies.

Since the program was started in 1996 over 600 candidates have interned with Entry Point! partners, and of that number, 85 percent are now working as scientists and engineers. That's a pretty great success rate.

So what are the requirements to apply? Candidates must have a disability, which can be either apparent or nonapparent (a statement of disability will be required). They must have a grade point average over 3.0, must be a US citizen, and they must be enrolled as a full-time undergraduate or graduate student. A couple of letters of recommendation will also be required.

As for companies that Entry Point! works with, well, NASA is one. Others include IBM, Merck, Dow Chemical, Lockheed Martin, Ball Aerospace, and L'Oréal, along with many university-based research programs, and there are sites located throughout the United States.

As an engineering lead for the Marshall Space Flight Center, Vicky considers herself exceptional at multitasking, a critical skill for being a good leader. Vicky has worked on all sorts of cool projects, including elements of the International Space Station. Currently working as a team lead, she now gets to focus on coordinating problem-solving efforts. When the team is faced with problems, how do they solve them? Do they fix the current solution? Look for alternative solutions? Vicky loves analyzing models and seeing how different scenarios might play out. And even though Vicky misses the more hands-on work, she also recognizes that with more responsibility, she also has more influence. And she can work to break down barriers in STEM.

As a leader, a woman, and a deaf person, Victoria Garcia faces many challenges. She notes that when a boy gets an equation wrong, someone may tell him that he is bad in math. When a girl gets that same equation wrong, it may be implied that "girls are bad at math." It's not fair, but it is one of the biases that some girls face when considering STEM fields.

How does Vicky solve this? She stays extra on top of her game, and, as she learned back in college, she speaks up for herself. Vicky recalls working with a guy that reported in to her. Every time she would ask for his status on a certain topic, he would dodge the question, over and over, until Vicky finally wrote what she considers a rather harsh email, letting him know that he needed to answer the question.

His response? He told Vicky that she was being very pushy. Would this have been his same response if his manager had been a man? It's doubtful. But by getting more female leaders and role models like Victoria Garcia in the workplace, these are the kind of biases we can change.

Vicky realizes that being deaf is her most obvious difference, but she also realizes that it places on her the responsibility of being a role model for others. For example, Vicky hates public speaking, and yet she does it because it makes a difference. After one public speaking event, a deaf student came up to her afterward and said, "I didn't know that deaf people could work for NASA."

"Yes!" Vicky says. "Deaf people can most definitely work for NASA."

Vicky herself had a very important role model growing up. The only famous person Vicky had ever seen who was deaf was the actress Marlee Matlin, but Marlee Matlin signed and did not communicate in the same way as Vicky. But when Heather Whitestone won the Miss America pageant in 1995, Vicky found the role model she had always wanted. Though Vicky had never wanted to be a beauty pageant contestant (she says she was quite the tomboy), she had finally found a famous person who communicated the same way she did. Vicky wants to be that role model for others, and she is doing a pretty amazing job.

Imagining the Invisible

Deep space has unlimited possibilities for exploration and discovery, and engineers are always looking for new ways to gather information. Take the work that Katie Bouman, electrical engineer and computer scientist, did with the Event Horizon imaging team at the Harvard-Smithsonian Center for Astrophysics. The team had an impossible objective: take a picture of a black hole. But wait! Black holes weren't even proved to exist. They were based on Einstein's theory of relativity, and the whole idea of a theory is that it's something that's not proven to be true. So how was taking a picture of a black hole going to be possible? To the nonscientist, this might sound a bit like capturing an image of the elusive Big Foot or a mythical unicorn, but for Katie Bouman and her team, this was an exciting opportunity to use their technical skills to get one step closer to proving Einstein's theory of relativity.

Capturing an image of a black hole isn't as easy as pointing a high-resolution camera at the sky and taking a picture. It's an image reconstructed from an enormous amount of data. How much data? Petabytes, to be precise. Let's put that into perspective. Your computer hard drive may have a terabyte of memory. That's considered a lot these days. A petabyte is 1,000 times bigger than that. Imagine having enough data to fill 1,000 computers. The hard drives alone that stored the data for the Event Horizon project weighed about 1,000 pounds!

Processing that much data required an intricate algorithm. It also required over 200 scientists dedicated to the task. Katie led a team to develop an algorithm to process all that data. The algorithm would reconstruct an image of the black hole. Known as continuous high-resolution image reconstruction using patch priors (or CHIRP, for short), it processed data collected from telescopes all over the world.

Scientists have to work hard to make sure their findings are correct, so the Event Horizon team broke up into groups, each doing independent research and developing their own algorithms. They weren't allowed to share data with each other. That way, they could ensure they weren't influencing other teams. Katie's team worked on their image and began to discover the existence of a ring around the black hole. But would other teams find the same thing? It turned out they did. On April 10, 2019, the image of the black hole was revealed. The teams worked together, compared data, and examined the results. The black hole existed, and there was a ring around it, like the Eye of Sauron. They had a picture to prove it.

As for the main message Vicky would love to get across to young girls? Don't be afraid of new experiences. Just try them. And when you try new things, you may find out something about yourself that you never realized before. You may get new opportunities. Your comfort zone will grow. And you will come to realize that you can do so much more than you ever imagined.

Shayna Begay:
Stand Strong

Have you ever seen the Milky Way in its full glory? On a Navajo reservation, basic utilities, like electricity and water, can be spotty. And Internet? That's a whole other challenge. Yes, having spotty electricity no doubt has its annoyances, but the benefits of low to no electricity means there is no light pollution. And no light pollution is what allowed Shayna Begay to first observe dark and beautiful skies from a very young age. It allowed her to see the Milky Way stretched across the sky like a Van Gogh painting. And it was magnificent. This was just one thing that paved the path for Shayna Begay to become a Native American female aerospace engineer.

The path to college was not handed over to Shayna easily. Her mother was Jewish, from New York, and her father was Navajo, from a reservation. They met in college in Arizona, got married, and moved to a reservation on a border town. Though both her parents dropped out of college their senior year, Shayna always knew the value of higher education because her parents and extended family had always emphasized how important it was. But she'd never even heard the word *engineer* until high school.

In early elementary school, Shayna was not the child who did well on timed math tests. In fact, she struggled . . . a lot. Her third-grade teacher saw her struggling and said something to Shayna's mom. Though Shayna's mom had dropped out of college, she worked as an accountant and was very good at math. She stepped in and started tutoring her daughter (along with other kids too). Both Shayna's mom and the teacher knew Shayna could do better. And with the right support at the right time, Shayna gained confidence and excelled at math.

Fast forward to middle school. Shayna was doing much better at math. She loved science. A vacation to Meteor Crater in Arizona only more firmly planted her love of outer space in her mind. One day her history teacher placed a piece of paper on her desk. It was an application for the astronaut program at NASA. He told her, "I think you're going to need this one day." He believed in her future, and by doing so, it helped Shayna believe in her future.

What Are the Best Places to Observe the Milky Way?

Look up into the night sky, and if there are no clouds out, you may be able to see around 2,000 stars. That sounds like a huge amount, but it barely breaks the ice of the full plethora of stars in the Milky Way. The Milky Way is the galaxy we live in, and it consists of between 100 and 400 billion stars. Now that is a lot of stars! But most people rarely if ever see the Milky Way in all its true glory.

So, when is the best time to see the Milky Way, and where are the best places in the United States to see it? First, you'll want to make sure it's the right time of year. For North America, that would be in the summer months, from about June to August. Yes, it's still in the sky during the other months, but it's much lower on the horizon and won't make for as spectacular of an experience. Also, you'll want to plan on viewing it when the moon is not in the sky. A great time for this is during the new moon phase. You can also plan your viewing for before the moon has risen or after it has set.

Clear skies are also important. True, you can't control the weather, but you can check it ahead of time. If the skies are going to be filled with clouds, you may want to delay your Milky Way viewing adventure until the weather clears up.

You'll want to go somewhere very dark to see it. This means away from cities and light pollution. The eastern United States has much more light pollution, but in the West, there are many locations you could visit. Bosque Del Apache National Wildlife Refuge in New Mexico is one of the top choices as no lights are allowed in the park. Natural Bridges National Monument in Utah offers not only darkness but also majestic backdrops with the huge stone arches. And if you are set on the eastern half of the United States, Cherry Springs State Park in Pennsylvania is a rare treat, offering amazing views.

One of Shayna's favorite grandparents would tell her to "reach for the sky . . . to infinity and beyond," and that is just what Shayna did as she started pursuing her future in STEM. (And yes, *Toy Story* was the inspiration behind those quotes. Oftentimes kids' movies have just the right message if we are willing to listen.) Even Shayna's mom would join in, telling Shayna to "reach high and go as far as you can." One day, Shayna decided to turn this back on her mom. She challenged her mom to go back to college and finish her accounting degree, and that is just what Shayna's mom did.

Once Shayna got to high school, she discovered her true goal. She wanted to be an engineer. After many science fairs, science camps, and even an engineering camp in Colorado, her dreams were planted in her brain. Now she just needed to find a way to make them come true.

Shayna's family did not have money for college, but her dad saw an article in the *Navajo Times* about the Bill and Melinda Gates Foundation and how they had scholarships available. He encouraged Shayna to apply for a scholarship, and she was accepted as a Gates Millennium Scholar. College was not just a dream anymore. It was a reality. Shayna went on to receive both her bachelor's and master's degrees in aerospace engineering from Florida Institute of Technology.

Mary Golda Ross

Mary Golda Ross was the first known Native American female engineer. In addition to that, she was also the first female engineer to work at Lockheed. Born in 1908 in Oklahoma, she was the great-granddaughter of Cherokee Chief John Ross. Mary Ross enrolled in college when she was sixteen and continued on to receive her bachelor's degree followed by her master's degree in mathematics. After getting hired by Lockheed, she began working on aircraft design for a secret project within the company called Skunk Works. After World War II she received her professional certification in aerospace engineering.

While at Skunk Works, she worked on preliminary design ideas for interplanetary travel, orbiting satellites, and both crewed and uncrewed Earth-orbiting flights. Beyond that, her engineering skills were put to use working on rocket design and ideas for missions to Venus and Mars.

After retiring, she worked to recruit young women and Native American youth into engineering fields.

So are outreach programs helping to help draw more Native American females into science and engineering? According to a study done by Sandia National Laboratories, only 1 out of 13,000 in the engineering workforce is a Native American or Alaska Native female. That's a pretty low percentage (0.007 percent which, just to make sure you're reading it correctly, is not even a hundredth of a percent). According to a study done by the National Science Foundation in 2005, just over 1,700 bachelor's degrees were awarded to Native American and Alaska Native females. Ten years later, in 2014 the number was roughly the same. We need to do better. Improving access and providing more opportunities can help, as can increasing the number of role models. It's important for every kid who looks to the stars and dreams of doing big things one day has the opportunity to achieve that future.

Shayna now works at Sandia National Laboratories as a rocket surgeon. OK, that's not her official title. Her official title is a principal member of technical staff, but Shayna equates her job to that of a surgeon's. Essentially, her team takes aging nuclear weapons and refurbishes them. It's like trying to extend the life of an old car without being able to drive it. Nuclear testing was banned in the 1990s, so the weapons can't actually be tested. These nuclear weapons were developed decades ago, but Shayna and her team need to keep them running as safely and securely as possible. So instead of actually testing them, they must find other means to verify the weapons will function properly. This is where the title "rocket surgeon" comes in. It's like doctors coming in and doing a checkup to make sure the weapons are healthy and safe. Shayna and her team need to monitor the health of the weapons over time, much as a doctor performs checkups on patients on a regular basis. This prevents accidents and prolongs the security force that helps protect our nation every day. Shayna says her job gets her out of bed each morning and makes her feel very proud to go to work each day.

In addition to being whip smart, Shayna is also a leader . . . of hundreds of people! Not everyone has the skill set to lead so many people so well, and as a woman, it comes with extra challenges, but Shayna has the secret. She believes more women should give themselves permission to fail. Women put a lot of pressure on themselves right out of the gate. They often feel like they need to do everything perfectly all the time.

This is not the case. It is OK to fail.

Yes, failure can be embarrassing and uncomfortable. It can put you in a weird position. But Shayna encourages those she leads and mentors to take the attitude that, "Now, we know we need to do something different. Here is what we learned. Here is what we can do better." In short, roll with it and keep moving forward. She encourages her team members to try new things and express new ideas. In doing so, not only will people learn faster, they will become more integrated with the team overall.

Feel like you have a voice and an opinion, and feel free to share it. Be willing to fail. Everyone, but females especially, need to be willing to get out there and be heard. Sometimes females are too nice and considerate. But they need to speak out and share their opinions because sometimes those opinions are the right solution to a problem. If you don't speak up, that solution or answer may never be found. And yes, you may fail when you do this. But that's OK. Don't be afraid to fail.

Shayna Begay is actively involved in many outreach programs, both through her employer, Sandia Labs, and on the reservation. The Dream Catchers Science Program is a STEM program sponsored by Sandia Labs as part of their American Indian Outreach Committee and is aimed at middle school and high school students. It's a great program that gets kids involved in hands-on science and engineering activities. Shayna is also on the engineering advisory board at Navajo Technical University. Shayna wants to help bring better education to the Navajo people as well as other indigenous people. She believes we need to improve resources and access, and set the bar higher for indigenous students, especially in the areas of STEM. Shayna also encourages girls to get involved in the Society of Women Engineers and the American Indian Science and Engineering Society, which she was able to join as young as middle school.

Mathematics and the Navajo Nation

At first glance, it might not seem like a woven rug has anything to do with mathematics, but take a deeper look. The patterns we see on these rugs not only tell stories; they visually portray mathematics. Navajo women instill the love of mathematics in children from a very young age, in so many ways. When a Navajo woman weaves a rug, she first estimates the lengths of yarn that will be needed based on where the rug will go. Depending on the pattern she plans to weave, she must arrange her various colored yarns in the correct manner. Then she weaves complicated symmetric geometric patterns that, though ornamental in appearance, have been well thought out and crafted. But learning the skills to be a rug weaver goes beyond mathematics. It teaches how to visualize a project and execute a plan from start to finish. It teaches patience for the things that take time, and how to fix mistakes when they are made. It teaches how to break down complex problems into smaller pieces. Think you'd like a Navajo rug? Be prepared to pay a pretty penny for it. An authentic Navajo rug can be pricey. Also make sure to watch out for fakes.

Mathematics doesn't stop at rugs in the Navajo Nation. Mathematical concepts are blended into woven baskets and wood carvings. Ratios are used, designs are rotated, and complex shapes are created. Today, computer programs are available to help in the design and planning of crafts such as these, and there are all sorts of lesson plans for classrooms to use, linking math and Navajo art. But for a child who's grown up in the Navajo Nation, this unique way of learning math they've observed from a young age can carry over and help them view STEM fields through a diverse lens.

Shayna also thinks back to those early role models in her life—her third-grade teacher, her mom, who tutored her, the history teacher who encouraged Shayna to dream big. Where would her life be without those role models? It's impossible to say. But the truth is clear. In order to attract more females from all backgrounds into STEM fields, we need more role models . . . like Shayna Begay. Reach for the stars. Dream big. And find a job that makes you excited and proud to get out of bed each day.

Appendixes

Appendix A

So You Want to Be an Engineer or a Coder?

I hope you've enjoyed all these inspiring stories about female coders and engineers jumping over hurdles and doing great things. I had so much fun talking with each and every one of these woman and hearing about their lives. Hearing some of these stories was such a step outside the life I knew and the life I had growing up, and I was thrilled to grow emotionally by the experience and be able to view the world through the lens of another.

Growing up, I always knew I wanted to be an engineer, but where do you fall on the spectrum? I hope you believe that being an engineer or a coder (or hey, maybe both!) is a possible future for you. I truly believe that so many more women could get into technical fields than currently do.

So let's say that you are inspired! You want to be an engineer or a coder. The number-one thing you're going to want to do is make a plan. Here's the thing about making a plan. Don't think that just because you've written something down you have to stick with it forever. Plans can be amended as needed. So make your plan. Maybe you write it out in a notebook. Maybe you type it on the computer. Wherever it is, make sure it's something that is easy to access and update. A plan that is written on a piece of paper and tucked away in a junk drawer may never see the light of day again (and neither may your goal). So open up that notebook or blank word processing page and get planning.

Do Something Today

The first thing you'll want to do is figure out what you can do RIGHT NOW that will get you closer to your dreams. Some possible options:

- **Sign up for a coding class.** Most schools offer coding classes, but if your school doesn't, talk to your counselor to see what your options might be. If you are in middle school, there might be an option to take a class at the high school. If you are in high school, then maybe a dual-credit course with a local community college will work. If none of those are options, look for an online class you can take. If you don't find a class the first time you look, don't give up. There are options out there.

- **Join a coding or robotics club.** It may add comic relief to television shows to have there be only one girl on a robotics team with a group of nerdy guys, but it does nothing to help get rid of the stereotype. Break the stereotype yourself. Throw out all those images you have from media of nerdy coding or robotics clubs, and sign up. Don't be shy or afraid to be the only girl there. Who knows? Maybe when you sign up, you will inspire other females to join also. These same females may have held back on joining because of the same stereotypes that held you back. We talked a lot about role modeling. This is your chance to be a role model.

- **Sign up for an engineering class.** Many schools have some kind of engineering classes available for students to take. Back when I was in school, a course many kids would take when they wanted hands-on experience with the world was shop. It taught the basics of how cars work along with many other useful skills like woodworking and how to use all sorts of power tools. These days, in schools, the equivalent of this class is often called engineering concepts. Remember, there are all types of engineers doing all sorts of jobs. If your school has a class like this, see if you can fit it in your schedule. Everything you learn in the class may not be exactly what you want to do with your life, but you are bound to be exposed to a lot of great new ideas and ways to tackle problems.

- **Take math and science courses.** If you do want to go into coding or engineering, a great thing to do right now is to look at your math and science classes and make sure you are challenging yourself enough. Don't overload yourself with coursework, but also don't just take the bare minimum. For those in high school, if you are taking one science class, it is possible to take a second? Many high schools offer courses like astronomy and environmental sciences. Can you supplement your science and math with online learning? Challenge yourself without stressing yourself out. You can do this!

- **Take something apart.** OK, this one might not be quite so popular with your family, so maybe you should ask first, but is there something you can take apart around your house and look inside? Maybe there's something that no longer works. A broken remote control? An exercise bike that no longer keeps track of cycles? A broken DVD player that's been sitting out in the garage since you were born? One thing about engineers is that they love to see how things work. When something is broken, it's like an open invitation to fix it. What's the worst that's going to happen? The item's already broken. Chances are your family will eventually put it in the trash can, so take your opportunity now. For most items you just need a Phillips head screwdriver, and you can get it open. That said, it's always a good idea to do an Internet search first. Some items, like a microwave oven, can be especially dangerous to work on (though often items of this sort have unique screws that can only be taken out with specialty screwdrivers).

Plan for College

Say it right now with me. "College is an option." Too often college is taken out of the realm of possibilities. Either it's not encouraged by parents, or it's deemed "impossible" owing to cost or other factors. But . . . college is an option. In your mind, it's important to plan to go to college if you want to be a coder or an engineer. Make that your plan and then figure out how you will achieve it.

We talked earlier about college and funding options, so we won't reiterate that here. What we will talk about is sticking to your plan. It may be the case that when you tell friends or family of your plans to go to college, they laugh or tell you that you aren't smart enough or that it will never happen. Think of these people like sea monsters. Back in the old days, when map makers were drawing maps of the world, they didn't know what lay beyond the known world. So what they would draw would be water with sea monsters. The idea was to tell anyone reading the map to stay away from the sea monsters. If you have sea monsters in your life who are telling you that your dreams aren't possible, don't listen to their negativity. They may be jealous. They may enjoy seeing others fail. Whatever the reason, they should be ignored.

Now say it with me again. "College is an option."

Ask for Help

There is no shame in asking for help to reach your dreams. Maybe it's advice on what courses to take that will best help your future. Maybe it's wondering if you should sign up for an SAT prep course. Maybe it's wondering how to navigate an application fee for a program when you don't have any money. Think of each of these things as trees that have fallen across the road. In order to keep driving, the tree needs to be moved out of the way. However, the tree is too big to lift all on your own. But if you and someone else move it together, it will be out of the way and you can be back on the path.

Counselors and teachers are an excellent source of knowledge. Is there a teacher you feel especially connected to? Talk to them if you need advice. It can be hard to summon up the courage to not only ask for help but to share our dreams for the future. But if you don't do these important steps, your chances of success will diminish.

Another important area to ask for help is when it comes time for college applications. Maybe colleges require essays to be written by potential students. Here's the thing about writing. All writers need editors. There is even a wonderful editor who worked with me on this book, making it as good as it could possibly be. Once you write an essay (and yes, you should definitely write it yourself), ask for help in editing it and proofreading it. Getting someone qualified to help make your essay shine will increase your odds of achieving the future you want.

Research Colleges

Yes, schools like MIT and Harvard are amazing, and it would be fantastic to go to one of them, especially on a full scholarship. That said, this is often not the case. OK, it would be more accurate to phrase that as it is almost always not the case. The vast majority of coders and engineers do not go to Harvard and MIT. They go to one of the thousands of other colleges across the country. So many of these colleges have excellent educational opportunities, and they should not be discounted just because they are not "one of the big schools" or "the school that my parents want me to go to."

It's a great idea to get online and do your research. Do you like snow? Maybe you want to go to college in Colorado.

Do you love the sunshine? What about Florida or Texas? It's a great idea to NOT set your sights on one college and one college alone. Pick between five and ten schools where you would be very happy going, and then do your research to see which ones feel like they might be a great fit for you.

Change Your Language

The language we hear growing up often becomes the language we speak. I'm not talking about a specific language like English, Spanish, or French. What I'm really talking about is the things we say.

Have you ever caught yourself saying, "I'm not good at math" or "Math is so hard"? This is the kind of language that should be eliminated. First of all, math is not so hard. And second, you can learn to be good at math.

What about things like "I play nerdy computer games" or "I like dorky movies." This is also language that can stop. The computer games you play are not nerdy, and you saying they are will only keep the (inaccurate) stereotype alive. The movies you love to watch are not dorky. They are cool and explore all sorts of great creative ideas.

Your language is often the language you grew up hearing, but if you can break the pattern right now, you can help pave the way for a better future. If you have a friend who says that math is hard, don't be afraid to call her out on it. Ask her why she thinks it is hard. See if you can help. Change the language for yourself and others.

Adapt

Things don't always work out like we plan. That's why, even though we start with a plan, it's great to remain flexible. Maybe your family decides to move across the country for a parent's job. That could change the list of potential colleges you might attend. Maybe you transfer schools and your new school doesn't offer the selection of math and science courses that your old school did. It might require you to start doing more online. The key thing here is don't panic! Don't give up. You can amend your plan.

For any plan you have in life, it's a great idea to revisit it every couple of months or so. How are you doing in working toward it? What changes need to be made? Make the necessary changes and start working toward your dreams once again!

Appendix B

Types of Engineers

When people think of engineers, the first thing that comes to mind may be people who build bridges. Yes, this is one type of engineering (civil engineering), but there are so many more types of engineers out there. Depending on what interests you and what you enjoy doing, you can find the perfect engineering field.

There are five main types: mechanical, electrical, industrial, chemical, and civil. Each of these types of engineering has many subcategories. Let's take a look at what some of the main categories and subcategories of engineering are.

Mechanical Engineering

Do you like designing machines? Mechanical engineering might be the right choice for you. Here are some of the sub-categories of mechanical engineering:

- Aerospace engineering
- Robotics
- Nanotechnology

If you love the idea of space, and think that you'd like to design transportation vehicles that fly, then maybe aerospace engineering is the right choice for you. Maybe you even want to be an astronaut. Aerospace engineering could be a good step in the right direction for that.

Possibly you love your Alexa and your Roomba, and you want to design robots of your own. Robotics is a great field to consider. So many things are robots—things you may not have even thought of. A robot is simply a machine that is designed to do tasks quickly and correctly. Your washing machine is a robot, and so is your coffee maker. Why not look around your house right now and see how many devices you can find that could be considered robots? But don't think if you go into robotics, you'll be working on the next best espresso machine (though that would be fantastic!). Rescue robots, which are robots that go on search-and-rescue missions, are a very cool field of robotics where your efforts could make a difference. Surgical robots are another area with the potential to save lives. Robots can make our lives easier and make a difference.

What about nanotechnology? Nanotechnology is the use of matter on an atomic scale for manufacturing and industrial purposes. Nano is a metric measurement for something that is really small (a billionth of a meter), hence the name. For perspective, a human hair is about 50,000 nanometers wide. Nanotechnology is currently in use in products such as food, cosmetics, and medicine to help keep us safe and protect our environment.

What about nanobots? You've almost certainly heard the term, but what are they? Technically, they fit more into the robotics arm of mechanical engineering, since a nanobot is a very small self-propelled machine. Research is being done to use nanobots in many fields, including the medical field. They have the potential to drastically improve many medical conditions including cancer and cell repair.

Electrical Engineering

Are you more interested in electricity and what makes computers run? If so, then electrical engineering might be in your future. There are all types of electrical engineers that do many different kinds of things. Subcategories for electrical engineering include the following:

- Computer engineering
- Power engineering
- Telecommunications
- Robotics

Computer engineering (my background) is a great field if you love computer programming and you think like an engineer. So much of our technology is made of up computers, and it's computer engineers that work behind the scenes on all that.

They work on both the hardware and the software behind the systems that keep our computers running. All those tiny chips inside cell phones? They're designed by computer engineers. The circuit boards inside our video game controllers? Also computer engineers. The future for computer engineering is bright!

If computer engineers design our computers, power engineers make sure we have the power to run them. During a winter storm a couple of years ago, the power grid in Texas nearly collapsed. Until this time, most people didn't know this was even a possibility. People didn't understand and were just outraged that there were rolling blackouts. But if not for power engineers warning that the power grid could collapse unless power was conserved, the entire grid could have gone off-line, causing power outages that may have lasted months. Power engineers also deal with renewable energy, a great area for anyone to consider. Fossil fuels are bad for the environment and also won't last forever. But renewable energy can keep our cell phones charged and our coffee makers brewing long after fossil fuels are gone.

And speaking of cell phones, a great subcategory of electrical engineering is telecommunications. Do you like your cell phone? Me too. Good thing a telecom engineer made it possible to send and receive satellite signals. Do you enjoy Internet at your house or the local Starbucks? Telecom engineers make sure the fiber coming into our homes and businesses works and gets us the fastest data rate (perfect for streaming all our favorite shows).

And what about that fourth one on the list: robotics? We just mentioned that under mechanical engineering. Here's the thing. Robots have moving parts (the mechanical parts), and they also have electrical parts. That's where the electrical engineer would come in. If you want to work on robots, you could be one of many types of engineer.

Industrial Engineering

If you think using many different skills to design systems sounds interesting, then industrial engineering might be the best choice. Industrial engineers come up with processes to make things operate better, faster, cheaper—whatever the constraint might be—and they can work in pretty much any field, include healthcare, manufacturing, supply chain, and quality assurance.

One way to think about industrial engineering is this: Have you ever had to do some kind of repetitive task around the house? Maybe you had to put away dishes or fold laundry. Maybe you wanted to reorganize your makeup drawer so the products you use the most are the easiest to get to. For dishes, you may find that it's easiest to put away all the plates first followed by all the bowls and then all the glasses. Or you may find that it's easiest to unload everything onto the counter and then put them away from there. Every kitchen will have a different best solution. The same is true with different products and manufacturing plants. It's up to industrial engineers to come up with the processes that work best for the environment they are working in. So the next time you think in your mind of the best process to do something, you're thinking like an industrial engineer!

Chemical Engineering

You might be more interested in physics and microbiology. If so, chemical engineering might be in your future. Chemical engineers combine science and engineering to work in areas such as medical research, pharmaceuticals, food processing, and the development of industrial chemicals.

In the medical field, they may look at the chemicals we are made of (yes, we are made entirely of chemicals!) and study how medications interact with them. They may look at the foods we eat and better engineer chemicals used to preserve them, making them healthier. Or perhaps they're working on the fertilizers when foods are grown, making sure they are not harmful to us or the environment. They may find chemicals to treat insects without harming pets. They may develop cleaning chemicals that won't degrade materials. They may design fibers that can be woven into our clothes, making our leggings stretchy enough to exercise in.

What about gas and oil? This is often the first thing we think of for chemical engineers, and yes, this is an area of research. Chemical engineers look at these petrochemicals and determine how they can be used most effectively with the least impact on the environment.

Civil Engineering

The environment leads us into the last main category of engineering: civil engineering. Yes, civil engineers design and build bridges, but they do so much more than that. Look at the world around you. There are roads, buildings, bridges, dams, tunnels, and water systems. Civil engineers work on all these things, making sure our society is built with safe infrastructure. If it is a major transportation project, then a civil engineer is behind it.

If you've sat in an airplane on the runway, waiting to take off, you've noticed the bevy of vehicles zipping around, seeming to go in all sorts of directions. Their movements aren't random, however. Everyone at the airport is following a well-orchestrated plan, from the gate controllers to the baggage handlers.

Civil engineers also work closely with the environment, trying to make the world as sustainable as possible. They look at water and chemical runoff from plants. They study pollution and come up with solutions to how to minimize it. They design our sewers and our wastewater treatment plants (most likely with the help of chemical engineers making sure the water is treated properly).

Niche Engineering

Just because there are five main branches of engineering doesn't mean you're stuck with one of these. There are some cool niche types of engineering degrees you could consider:

- **Biomedical engineering.** It's like biology, chemistry, and engineering mashed together. Biomedical engineers often work in healthcare and medical research.

- **Mining engineering.** If you like minerals, digging in the earth, and geology, then mining engineering is a solid option. Mining engineers work to keep damage to the surrounding areas of mining operations to a minimum.

- **Nuclear engineering.** If the idea of safe nuclear power is something that interests you and you crave to learn more about the atom, then nuclear engineering has it all. Nuclear engineers help protect the environment while working to provide a solid source of energy.

- **Agriculture engineering.** Food should be tasty, healthy, and not harmful to the earth. An agriculture engineer will work on the design of equipment and plants where food is processed, making sure it's handled properly from seed to table.

- **Interdisciplinary engineering studies.** If you love the idea of engineering, but you aren't quite sure what type of engineer to be, then a more general degree is a great option. In the interdisciplinary engineering studies path, you'll have flexibility to create your own plan of study.

The next time someone tells you that they're an engineer, ask them what kind they are and what they do. It might be the perfect kind of engineering for you too. After all, engineering means problem solving, and that is something that everyone has the talent to do!

Appendix C
Cool Programming Jobs

You love computer programming, but maybe you aren't so sure you want to work for a big tech company. Don't worry. There are so many other choices and cool jobs when it comes to programming, many of which might tie into one of your interests or hobbies. Before you settle for a job you don't like or that you think will be monotonous, why not take a step back and see if there is some kind of perfect programming job out there that combines the best of both worlds? After all, it's those jobs that draw in what we are really interested in that will help make us excited to get up and work each day. Your perfect job could be out there waiting for you. Or maybe it's a job you need to create yourself. Let's take a look at some of the fun and unique jobs in computer programming that go beyond the high-tech company.

Bioinformatics

Let's say you are fantastic at computer programming and you've always been fascinated by the human genome. There is a really cool field of study called Bioinformatics that could be right up your alley. The human genome (or really any genome for that matter) is huge. After all, a genome contains all the biological information to create a living thing. In the last years, there has been so much research on genomes and sequence identification. Just to wrap our minds around how much data we're working with, though, the human genome is about 6.4 billion base pairs long. That's such a big number that without the help of computers, it could never be analyzed. But with the help of computers, scientists are able to combine biology and computer science to analyze these vastly large amounts of data.

Computational Archaeology

Maybe instead of biology what you really love is archaeology. Archaeology has fascinated people for centuries, and when we think of the field, what often comes to mind is characters like Indiana Jones out in the desert looking for lost tombs and treasure. Finding treasure is not what the field is all about. Much of what archaeologists want to uncover is the long-term behavior of humans and how behavior has evolved. There's an exciting field called computational archaeology, or sometimes archaeoinformatics, where computers are used to analyze these long-term behaviors. Additionally, computers and programs can be used to re-create excavation sites and construct 3D models of pottery and other relics.

Video Game Designer

Is there any kid in America who hasn't played a video game of some sort? Whether it's solitaire, *Minecraft*, or *MarioKart*, video games are popular beyond belief and not going anywhere. A really creative and sought-after programming job is as a video game designer. If you've ever had a chance to tour a video game company, you'll realize that making video games takes an entire team of people. There are artists, animators, testers, writers, and of course, the programmers who are actually writing the code to run the game. If you're the kind of person who's considering modding your favorite game or gotten frustrated with game updates and releases filled with bugs, then maybe programming video games is your calling. It's fun, popular, and creative, and also—let's face it—sounds pretty cool.

Website Designer

For every website you've gone to—and let's face it, that is a ton—someone has designed that website. Unless the entire Internet collapses, which we all really hope won't happen, website design is going to be around for a long time. Companies, musicians, grocery stores all have websites. They want to make sure the pages load fast, are easy to update, and look snazzy enough to draw people back for return visits. Or maybe there is a company you want to start. You could have the greatest business idea ever. Without a website, your product will never get known, and a really fun way to start learning website design is to play with a website of your own.

Getting started with website design is easy. Standing out in website design will take work. But it's a great way to combine creativity with programming and deliver a product that customers will love.

Geoscientist

It could be the case that you love programming and you love geology. Geoscientists study the Earth to learn about its past, present, and future. That's great, but how does programming fit into all this? Go ahead and search the Internet for a simulation of how the continents formed and changed over time because of plate tectonics. Or search to see how they are predicted to change in the future. Look for simulations on the changes in the flow of rivers, in the rising of sea levels, in the formation of the Grand Canyon.

Programming makes all these simulations possible and more. It's one thing to go out on site and study rock samples, but it adds an entirely new skill set when those discoveries can be studied and expanded upon with computer simulations.

Robotics

We mentioned robotics when we looked at branches of engineering and found it could fit into quite a few different types of engineering fields. Another place robotics fit in is with computer programming.

Robots are computers that are programmed to do tasks. Mechanical engineers build the moving parts. Electrical engineers design the circuitry to make them operate. Chemical engineers may work on using the best materials for their intended purposes. And computer programmers write the code that instructs them how to do the tasks they are intended for.

There are many science-fiction stories about the lone genius who designs the perfect robot, but for the most part, this will remain in the realm of science fiction. Designing and building robots takes a team of people working together toward a common goal. Now, Alexa, wash the dishes.

Predicting the Future

Can computers be programmed to predict the future? It depends on what they're trying to predict. Programmers have written code to analyze videos of people performing certain actions, like cooking various recipes. The programs study which behaviors follow others, and using this information, the software predicts what will happen in the future.

How many repetitive tasks do we do each day? Are you such a creature of habit that if a computer studied your behaviors for a few days, it would then be able to predict what you would do next? Do you brush your hair before or after you brush your teeth? Do you always put your salad dressing on before or after sprinkling bacon bits over your lettuce?

Our brains fall into routines for how we do things, and with quite a bit of accuracy, a computer can predict what will happen next. Much of this programming is early in the stages of development, and predicting actions further than five minutes in the future becomes less certain. But it certainly opens up a whole new world of possibility for what computers will be able to do.

Does any of this sound interesting? Maybe! But if not, think of the things you love. Is it sports? Weather prediction? Amusement parks? Building things? One of the great things about computer programming is that it can be used in virtually any field of work. It can help with day-to-day activities or it can be the foundation for building a new business. Whatever the case, even if you decide to not major in computer science, learning basic coding skills will almost always be a benefit to your future career.

Appendix D
Books and Movies

After giving birth to my son, when I went back to work at my engineering job, I commuted to and from daycare a few times a day. I'd drop my son off in the morning. I'd visit at lunch to nurse him. And I'd pick him up in the evening. What this worked out to be was many, many hours in the car. In rush hour traffic. Every single day except weekends.

There are a handful of things you can do while driving. You can sit in silence. This is a great choice, especially if you are easily distracted. It's important to make focusing on the road the top priority. If you can handle some distraction, radio or music is one way to pass the time. I love music, and for many years I listened to it in the car while driving to and from work. But once I gave birth to my son and went back to worth, I started looking at all that time in the car as an opportunity to learn more. To read more. To expand my mind.

I got an audiobook subscription with Audible and since then I've listened to over 500 audiobooks. Listening to books offers a chance to read material you might otherwise not read. For my audiobook selections, I listen to a bunch of science fiction and fantasy, some recent popular fiction titles, and tons of nonfiction. In the nonfiction category, learning more about the world and about science expands my mind. In addition, I love books on personal development, on building and keeping good habits and getting stuff done. And I've also recently listened to some amazing titles looking at the world through the lens of a woman.

The world is historically different in the ways it treats women, and unless we recognize this and start speaking up, nothing will change. I'd love to challenge everyone reading this book to pick a nonfiction audiobook title and give it a listen. You may be surprised by the things you can learn and the ways your view of the world will change.

Below are some of my favorite audiobooks on female empowerment:

- *Brave, Not Perfect: Fear Less, Fail More, and Live Bolder* by Reshma Saujani
- *Burnout: The Secret to Unlocking the Stress Cycle* by Emily Nagoski and Amelia Nagoski
- *Drop the Ball: Achieving More by Doing Less* by Tiffany Dufu
- *Girl, Stop Apologizing: A Shame-Free Plan for Embracing and Achieving Your Goals* by Rachel Hollis

- *Girl, Wash Your Face: Stop Believing the Lies About Who You Are So You Can Become Who You Were Meant to Be* by Rachel Hollis
- *Lean In: Women, Work, and the Will to Lead* by Sheryl Sandberg
- *The Moment of Lift: How Empowering Women Changes the World* by Melinda Gates
- *The Power of Vulnerability: Teachings on Authenticity, Connection, and Courage* by Brené Brown
- *Weapons of Math Destruction: How Big Data Increases Inequality and Threatens Democracy* by Cathy O'Neil

In addition to audiobooks, I'm always up for a great movie with strong female characters, especially those who love designing things and using their brains. Movies are two hours of your time, so you might as well pick something you're going to enjoy and connect with. I know there are a ton more out there, but here are some of my favorite movies with strong, smart women:

- *Enigma* (2001)
- *Legally Blonde* (2001)
- *V for Vendetta* (2005)
- *Ghostbusters* (2016)
- *Hidden Figures* (2016)
- *Wonder Woman* (2017)

- *Black Panther* (2018)
- *Annihilation* (2018)
- *Lara Croft: Tomb Raider* (2018)

What movies and books do you love, and what are you inspired to read? Talk to your friends about it. See if you have similar tastes. If so, maybe you and a handful of friends want to read the same book and get together to talk about it. Book clubs aren't just for suburban moms. Anyone can join or form a book club. Make a plan of it. Figure out what you're going to read and where you're going to meet. Come up with some discussion topics ahead of time. Also get some snacks. Snacks make everything better. Then talk about the book. You may be amazed at what you get out of the book that your friends completely miss, or maybe it will be the other way around. Maybe they'll remind you of something you skimmed right over. And the best part? Together you can change the world.

Appendix E
All About Advanced Degrees

Going to college (and graduating!) is a huge accomplishment. But should the road of education be over after getting your undergraduate degree? Not necessarily. There are lots of factors to consider and some things you may want to know when it comes to getting the right education for being an engineer or a coder.

When someone out of high school goes to college for engineering or programming, it's going to take them about four years to get their degree. What they'll most likely end up with is a bachelor's in science (a BS, for short). This is such a wonderful accomplishment, and it should be celebrated. But then what comes next? Should you get a job or get more education? There are a few choices of what you can do.

First, the lure of making money is a strong one. When graduates are presented with the idea of starting salaries for engineering and programming positions, it seems like a ton of money. Taking a job is a great option! You may graduate from your four-year college and decide you've had enough of books and learning. If so, and if you've considered other options and decided they aren't right for you, then by all means, take this path.

However, a different choice you may want to make is to go directly to graduate school in engineering or programming. Many graduate programs take about two years, and at the end of these two years, you'll graduate with a master's of science (MS). By going to graduate school, candidates will often have the opportunity for better jobs at a higher starting salary. Companies may only want to consider candidates with graduate degrees. If the drive to make money as soon as possible isn't your top concern, then sticking around right after getting your undergraduate degree is a solid choice worth considering.

Now, let's say you graduate with your bachelor's and master's degrees. What comes next? Again, you could get a job, or you could stick around for even more school. Those who really enjoy research and learning may decide to pursue a PhD. This program will take a minimum of three more years and could be longer depending on how quickly you proceed through the program. A PhD is the highest degree you can achieve.

All that said, there are other paths and options. What if, for example, after graduating with your four-year undergraduate degree, you decide getting a job is the best option. You may land a sweet job with a fantastic salary . . . and then decide that you want the opportunities that a master's degree will offer. It's not too late! In fact, you have a couple of options at this point. You could take a leave of absence from your current job (or resign) and pursue your master's degree full-time. Obviously, you'd need a way to support yourself if this were the case since you wouldn't have the job. You could take out loans to help pay, borrow the money, or look for a job as a teaching assistant to help fund your degree. You could also work and go to school at the same time. This is a lot more common than you might think.

Many colleges offer flexible schedules and night courses for those students who are working and pursuing a higher degree. Check your local college and see what programs they offer. That said, to work and go to school at the same time is going to take some discipline. If you go this route, make sure you are committed to working hard. Much of your free time when not working will be spent studying and working on course work. Also, by doing both at the same time, getting your master's degree may take longer than the standard two years. That's OK, though. Stay committed to your course and see it through to the end.

There is also another option to consider. Just because your undergraduate degree was in engineering or programming does not mean you have to stick with that path forever. Getting a different type of degree, like an master's of business administration (MBA) or a master's in project management could be the right path and present you with better job opportunities in the future. For every engineering or programming project people may be working on, there is someone leading the charge. Someone needs to be making sure the schedules are met and the budgets abided by. It takes some people skills and technical skills to be a project manager, but it's also a great way to learn more about an entire project rather than just one piece.

All these decisions sound like a lot to think about. But don't let it overwhelm you. The important thing is to understand your options and to not jump into any decisions. Opportunities of all sorts will come your way. It's up to you to analyze each one and see if it falls on the path to where you want to be in life. And if you make one choice (like deciding to work right away instead of getting an advanced degree), don't feel like you can never change your mind. The world and the future are open to you. It's up to you to make the most of it!

Appendix F

How to Program the Great Pyramid

I know how things are. There are some of you out there right now reading this book, thinking things like "I don't like programming" or "I just don't understand how programming works." I'd love to invite you to take a step back and go on a little adventure with me while we look at just a few programming concepts.

Programming concepts are nothing new. They've been around for thousands of years. Maybe, we could say, since humans started solving problems. Don't believe me? Read on.

Something I love (besides engineering and coding) is archaeology. There is something about mysteries of the past that makes me want to learn as much as I can. For example, how did the Egyptians build the pyramids?

The pyramids are a pretty major engineering project. The Great Pyramid of Giza is the oldest and largest of the pyramids on the Giza site. It was one of the Seven Wonders of the Ancient World, and it's the only one still intact. At its base, it measures 755 square feet, and it's about 455 feet high. To put that in perspective, that's like two and a half football fields in each direction for the base, and for height, that's almost as tall as the Washington Monument. It's estimated that 2.3 million blocks were used in the construction. If you were the head architect in charge of building the Great Pyramid, you would want to make sure you did the job correctly and efficiently. Otherwise, the pharaoh might have you fed to the crocodiles or something equally terrible.

Moving that many stone blocks takes a plan. Making sure the proportions are correct takes precision. But you can't move every stone yourself. You need to make good directions that the workers moving the stones can follow. You might create instructions like:

(A) Repeat these steps until you reach the end of the row:

- Get a stone block (if would take a lot of people to move the stone block, but that's a whole different topic).
- Roll the stone block to the next open space and place it there.

This is a standard REPEAT UNTIL programming concept. It's a loop. You REPEAT instructions UNTIL a certain condition is met. In this case, the condition is reaching the end of the row. When the end of the row is reached, you stop this current loop.

(B) If you reach the end of the row:
- If all four sides are complete, then move to the next level
- Otherwise, turn right and start your (A) instructions from above once more.

This is a standard IF/THEN/ELSE programming concept. It's what's called a conditional statement. IF you reach the end of the row and IF all four sides are complete, THEN move to the next level ELSE turn right and start (A) once more.

(C) While you are using more than one stone per level:
- Keep building upward

This is a standard WHILE LOOP programming concept. Like the REPEAT UNTIL, it's a loop, but it is slightly different in how it operates. WHILE you are not at the top, keep building upward.

See, programming concepts are just logical. In fact, that's really what programming is about. Logic. And maybe you haven't built the Great Pyramid of Giza, but you've most likely done something else equally cool. What logic have you used recently?

Appendix G
On Writing *Problem Solvers*

Over the course of about six months, I had the incredible pleasure of interviewing these fifteen amazing female engineers and coders. It was exhilarating, fast-paced, stressful, and eye-opening, all at the same time.

Being on this side of the interview table (the virtual table) was an entirely new experience for me. In my job as an author, I've been interviewed many times, in person and virtually. I never really gave much thought as to what would be involved on the opposite side of the table. To say it was different is an understatement. Now that I've had that experience, I'd love to share a bit with you!

I'm an organized person, so I figured interviewing would be as simple as coming up with a list of women I'd love to feature, setting up the interviews, and then marking them off the list. No problem at all. But there were obstacles to overcome from the start. First, it turns out that not everyone has their e-mail listed online. Digging through trying to find contact information can be challenging. For some of the women, I could find no e-mails. For others, I found five e-mails! Some mentioned on their websites that they prefer to be contacted through a media person. Some needed to be contacted through the companies that they worked for. In short, for each of the fifteen women featured, the process to gather contact information varied. But I got the e-mails. I had contact information! Now, let's move on to the next obstacle.

I sent e-mails. Some responded right away. Some didn't respond at all. Sometimes people get busy. I sent follow-up e-mails. Responses came! The interviews were going to happen. We can thank the pandemic here a bit for making video communications so much more of a standard thing. Sure, there was Skype before, but now nearly everyone was using Zoom. I set up interview appointments with each of the fifteen women.

Then I crossed my fingers. Please let there be no power outages. No internet hiccups (Zoom loves to freeze up for a minute at a time and give the message "Your Internet Connection is Unstable"). No dogs barking in the background. No Amazon packages being delivered. Thankfully, when working with fifteen engineers and coders, technical issues were not a problem. Also, I wasn't the only one with barking dogs at home.

For each interview, I had a list of questions. I was prepared. What I wasn't prepared for was the golden nuggets hidden inside. The first interview I conducted was with Danielle Merfeld, VP and Chief Technology Officer of GE Renewable

Energy. I asked her my questions; she gave me answers. But so much more came out of it than that. There was a message inside: how one small action can change the path of your future. My next interview was with Gabriela A. González, Chair of the NSF STEM Education Advisory Panel. As she was telling me her story, I couldn't help but cry. By the end of the interview, we were both in tears. The obstacles she'd overcome to get to where she is today are astounding.

The next thirteen interviews were exactly the same. Each interview lasted about an hour. A couple went way longer. A handful were shorter. But I got so much more out of each one than I ever would have dreamed possible. And with the interviews now complete, I was ready to write the book.

I had these visions of listening to each interview again and taking notes. I'd recorded everything on Zoom after all. But after one interview, I realized what a tedious process this was going to be. So instead, a friend recommended a software tool called Otter.ai. I could import my audio file, and Otter would transcribe the interviews for me. Sure, it got a word wrong here or there, but for the most part, it was perfect. From these transcribed interviews, I wrote my book!

But wait. That's not the end of the process. When writing nonfiction, it's important to make sure nothing is misrepresented. I wanted to make sure I hadn't gotten a detail wrong or used a word choice that might cast someone or something in the wrong light. I e-mailed each chapter out to the interviewee for review.

In some cases, the women got down to the copyediting level for the chapters. In other cases, they fact-checked and made sure I correctly represented not only them but also the projects they were working on. In a few of the cases, the chapters had to be run by the human resources department for the company where they worked. We all wanted to make sure the information provided in the book was not only interesting but also factual. And for some of the companies, it was important that no security levels were breached.

I received the final chapter edits at midnight, the night before the manuscript was due to my editor. I got in the changes and sent it. It had finally all come together. Now it was a book.